KU-423-280

Car Theft: The Offender's Perspective

by Roy Light, Claire Nee and Helen Ingham

A HOME OFFICE
RESEARCH AND PLANNING UNIT
REPORT

LONDON: HMSO

© *Crown copyright 1993*
Applications for reproduction should be made to HMSO
First published 1993

ISBN 0 11 341069 7

HOME OFFICE RESEARCH STUDIES

'Home Office Research Studies' comprise reports on research undertaken in the Home Office to assist in the exercise of its administrative functions, and for the information of the judicature, the services for which the Home Secretary has responsibility (direct or indirect) and the general public.

On the last page of this report are listed titles already published in this series, in the preceding series *Studies in the Causes of Delinquency and the Treatment of Offenders*, and in the series of *Research and Planning Unit Papers*.

HMSO

Standing order service

Placing a standing order with HMSO BOOKS enables a customer to receive other titles in this series automatically as published.

This saves time, trouble and expense of placing individual orders and avoids the problem of knowing when to do so.

For details please write to HMSO BOOKS (PC11B/2), Publications Centre, P.O. Box 276, London SW8 5DT and quoting reference 25.08.011.

The standing order service also enables customers to receive automatically as published all material of their choice which additionally saves extensive catalogue research. The scope and selectivity of the service has been extended by new techniques, and there are more than 3,500 classifications to choose from. A specialist leaflet describing the service in detail may be obtained on request.

Foreword

Car crime has become a source of increasing concern recently. During Car Crime Prevention Year, it was appropriate to mount a study taking a detailed look at the perspective of those actually involved in stealing cars. The report gives us some useful insights into the reasons why young people get involved in car theft and how they might effectively be deterred or diverted. Their understanding and appreciation of legal sanctions as deterrents suggests that challenging non-custodial programmes may be more appropriate for those apprehended than either cautioning or custody.

The report is the product of a collaborative project, involving the Research and Planning Unit (Claire Nee) and the University of the West of England (Roy Light and Helen Ingham). All tasks in carrying out the study and preparing the report were shared equally between the Research and Planning Unit and the University. I very much hope we shall continue in such collaborative ventures.

ROGER TARLING
Head of Research and Planning Unit

Acknowledgements

We would like to thank the 100 respondents who took part in the research, for their time and honesty; and all those from probation services, NACRO training centres and motor projects who helped us gain access to them, particularly Gerry Beare, Dino Peros and Pete West.

We are greatly indebted to Pat Mayhew, for her comments, advice and input on several drafts of the report, and to Mike Hough who also helped. We would like to thank Dan Shephard for his help on pilot work, Natalie Aye Maung for help with the fieldwork, and David Heppenstall for help on the preparation of the report.

ROY LIGHT
CLAIRE NEE
HELEN INGHAM

Contents

Summary

The central aims of the present study were to look at the car crime 'career', to assess offenders' perceptions of criminal justice sanctions, and to investigate some of the situational factors that affect choice of targets. Semi-structured interviews were conducted with 100 car thieves aged between 14 and 35 living in a variety of places in England and Wales. They were located through motor projects, probation day centres and NACRO training centres. The social background of the sample reflected that of young offenders generally: low academic achievement, high unemployment, and restricted leisure activities. Those interviewed mostly said that their families were concerned about their level of offending but felt unable to intervene.

Most of the sample became involved in car crime in their early to mid-teens, when over two-thirds were still officially at school. Most had extensive careers in terms of both length of involvement and number of offences committed, offending at least two to three nights a week at their peak. Many had escaped contact with the police for much of their career. A fifth had never come to police notice at all. Involvement in other crime was not uncommon—including burglary, shoplifting, and ramraiding.

Initial involvement in car crime tended to be with other more experienced offenders and primary reasons for starting to steal cars were peer influence, boredom and potential excitement. A period of 'apprenticeship' lasted for around six months to a year, after which thieves became notably more skilled and confident. After this, for many, stealing cars became more than just a way of getting a thrill. As well as the money to be made from casual theft from cars, which was very common, just over a third of the sample went on to more organised profit-making, termed here 'professional' theft. This included stripping cars to sell the parts; giving them false identities for resale; selling them on to receivers; or destroying them for insurance purposes. A fifth of the sample, some of whom engaged in other professional car crime activities, also became ramraiders. As careers progressed, the opportunity for financial gain began to feature more prominently in motivations for offending, though excitement was clearly still a factor.

The findings suggest that excessive levels of car theft are more akin to an adolescent infatuation or obsession than to true compulsion or addiction. A strong degree of personal pay-off in terms of excitement, status and self esteem, from stealing cars was nevertheless evident, particularly for the very young offender.

Just over half of the sample considered themselves to be car crime 'specialists' concentrating more or less exclusively on stealing cars. They were characterised by an early passion for cars; early aspirations to legal car-orientated occupations; earlier illegal driving on the road; higher rates of offending; and longer experience of car crime.

A fifth of the sample claimed to have desisted from car crime for a reasonable length of time. They gave reasons of increased responsibility and maturity rather than the threat of custodial sentences for giving up. Nearly forty per cent of the sample were potential desisters—claiming to have given up in the last few weeks; they gave similar reasons for stopping as longer-term desisters.

While car parks appeared to be particularly vulnerable to car theft many offenders were not specific about where they stole cars from. Three types of cars seemed especially at risk: those which are considered easiest to steal, often older cars; familiar cars with which offenders feel comfortable; and performance/sporty cars which offenders would like to own if given the opportunity. Alarms appeared to be of some deterrent value, though otherwise vehicle security was reported as lamentably weak, with offenders easily overcoming door and ignition locks. The findings on Vehicle Watch were disappointing, endorsing the need for a full evaluation of current practice.

Despite an overwhelming view that stealing a car was wrong, most offenders did not consider it a serious offence, although there was some evidence that this was changing due to media coverage of deaths linked with car theft and to the introduction of increased penalties.

The vast majority of offenders had been chased by the police, though this was seen more as an occupational hazard than as a deterrent to theft or as likely to lead to being caught. A third did concede, however, that police chases were the worst thing about car crime; although for some chases provided a challenge and the opportunity to show off driving skills. The experience of serious accidents and fatalities appeared not to deter the car thief.

Most offenders gave little thought to the possibility of being apprehended, and did not feel they would be anyway. Asked about what punishment they might attract if they were caught, over half the sample said they did not think about this either—the figure being higher among younger interviewees. Among those who had speculated on likely penalties, the chance of a custodial sentence was grossly overestimated in terms of current sentencing practice. In contrast, the chance of being cautioned was underestimated, particularly by younger thieves. As well as cautioning being considered unlikely, so too were most other non-custodial disposals such as conditional discharge, probation and community service. And none of these sanctions was considered a deterrent. A quarter of those who expected a fine or driving ban saw this as a deterrent, though it is not possible to determine which penalty was the greater threat. Half of those who expected custody felt similarly, though there were indications that the idea of curtailment of liberty may be more potent than the actuality. Only one of the fourteen who had experienced custody admitted that this had made him stop.

When asked for their views on the Aggravated Vehicle-Taking Act 1992, just over half said the increased penalties might deter them, though a more important function of the Act may lie in changing offender perceptions as to the seriousness of car theft.

Policy implications

Perhaps the main requirement in diversionary disposals is to provide car thieves with a comparable degree of excitement and interest to that which they get from car theft itself (see below). In addition, though, diversionary disposals would seem to need a strong educational component, given that most offenders demonstrated a lack of understanding of the seriousness of car theft. Probation orders for instance may be most effective if they carry the condition to attend offending groups and/or motor projects. Also worth attention is concerted effort to educate those most at risk of becoming car thieves about the seriousness and social costs of offending.

Three distinctive features surrounding car theft were identified which may have implications for prevention. First, the excitement, status and enhanced self-esteem that follow from stealing cars—any form of intervention needs to keep this clearly in focus. Well-structured motor projects are likely to incorporate a strong element of 'thrill' and these are already being developed and operated by probation services and voluntary agencies. Evaluation of such projects is under way to identify best practice and assess crime reduction potential. Secondly, the considerable degree of specialism among those involved in car theft suggests that the early identification and diversion of these car-obsessed 'specialists' would make the most substantial inroad into reducing the number of offences committed. Thirdly, the ease of progression from casual and hedonistic involvement to more organised profit-making at a very early age further underlines the value of early intervention in the apprenticeship stage. The targeting of younger offenders seems critical.

Finally, in terms of situational prevention, the results carried messages for both manufacturers and car owners. One beneficial approach would be for manufacturers to introduce deadlocks as standard on all new cars. Some alarms seem to deter some offenders, though the relative efficiency of different makes and types need more investigation, with results made known to owners. The development of wheel protection for sought-after models would also seem helpful, as would action by the police to curtail outlets for the goods procured through car crime.

Action by manufacturers to provide better security on new cars will only benefit new owners, and some escalation of skills on the part of more determined thieves to surmount new devices cannot be ruled out. Owners of older cars—for whom greater risks might ensue as newer cars become better protected—have little option but to augment their existing car security and take heed of crime prevention advice as regards risky parking locations, and leaving valuables on display for instance.

1 Introduction

Amidst the overall increase in property crime recorded in England and Wales during the late 1980s and early 1990s there has been a particularly sharp rise in theft of and from cars. Added to this has been concern over disturbances in places such as Blackbird Leys, Oxford and the Meadow Well estate, North Shields in the summer of 1991 involving cars illegally taken, often by very young thieves, for 'hotting' or display driving. Media coverage of these events and some well-publicised fatal accidents involving young people in stolen vehicles has brought car crime sharply into public focus. New offences with increased penalties were introduced and 1992 was designated Car Crime Prevention Year, with a £5 million publicity campaign—'a war against the hooligans on wheels' as the then Home Secretary put it. At the time of writing (July 1992), disorder in Hartcliffe, Bristol triggered by the deaths of two young men riding a stolen police motorcycle, and reports in the press of young people killed in police pursuits, further underlined the need for effective policies to deal with car crime.

Although the problem is clearly not new—indeed the literature points to a long-standing relationship between young people and car crime throughout Western Europe and North America—there has been a relative scarcity of significant work on the subject notwithstanding some recent overviews (Home Office, 1988; Houghton, 1992; Webb and Laycock, 1992) and discussions of preventive options (Southall and Ekblom, 1985; Clarke, 1991). The present research was undertaken as a further contribution to policy debate, its principal focus being the behaviour of car thieves themselves.

Aims of the present study

A certain amount is now known about the demographics of the offender, and we know something of the cars they target and how they break in. But there are still quite large gaps in our knowledge. The most obvious is that of the car crime career—what are the circumstances surrounding offenders' initial involvement in car crime, what maintains it, do they grow out of it, is it related to and does it lead on to other types of offending? We need to know in more detail, too, about the general characteristics and social background of car offenders—are these typical young offenders or merely bored young people without much other criminal experience? Further, little is known about offenders' perception of the

1

risk of being caught or of punishment—which is of particular interest with the advent of the Aggravated Vehicle-Taking Act in 1992.

There is also a need for better information on the process of stealing cars, particularly as it relates to crime prevention issues, such as the deterrent value of alarms and the ease of overcoming locks. Alarms are especially important, as research results are mixed as to whether they deter, the extent of any displacement effect, and the relative merits of various types and makes of alarm.

Methodology

Semi-structured interviews were conducted on a one-to-one basis with 100 young people who were or had been involved in car theft offences. Aimed at avoiding the inconsistencies associated with the self-completion of question-naires, the interviews were designed to address specific topics, while allowing the interviewees room to expand upon issues and introduce specific topics of their own. The major drawback of such a methodolgy is, of course, that it is both time-consuming and resource-intensive—effectively limiting the number of interviews that can be conducted. However, despite the limitations of a sample size of 100, the interviews provided more detailed qualitative data than is generally available. An additional benefit is that the researchers were able to have direct contact with the sample, thus increasing confidence in the validity of the responses.

The fieldwork was carried out over the period January to April 1992. Interviews were conducted with a sample of 98 boys and two girls aged 14 to 35 with a history of car crime involvement.

Selection of sample

The majority of the sample was located through motor projects and probation day centres; others came through bail hostels, NACRO training centres and other day or training centres for juveniles. Most were from the lower socio-economic groups: those who often find themselves on the receiving end of the criminal justice system. The study is therefore uninformative on car offending within other social groups. Similarly, although some of the sample taken from motor projects, youth centres and community arts projects had avoided formal contact with the criminal justice system, the study is recognised as being biased towards apprehended offenders. It may therefore say little of relevance to those skilful or lucky enough to avoid getting caught. Further, as many thieves came from rehabilitation projects, it may overrepresent offenders thought more suited to such programmes than others.

The research sites[1], spread throughout England and Wales, fall into five geographical areas (Table 1.1).

---

[1] Batley, Birmingham, Bristol, Cardiff, Frome/Wells, Leicester, London, Manchester, Newcastle-upon-Tyne, Oxford, Plymouth, Port Talbot, Swansea, Swindon, and Telford.

Table 1.1
Areas from which sample selected (n = 100)

	n
Midlands	21
North of England	32
South Wales	15
South West	22
Thames Valley	10
Total	100

Sample age

Criminal Statistics show the vast majority of apprehended vehicle offenders to be male and the peak age for offending to be between 14 and 20 years. To chart changes through this range the sample was grouped for the purpose of analysis by age (Table 1.2).

Table 1.2
Age of sample (n = 100)

	n
14	1
15–16	21
17	23
18–20	24
21–25	24
over 25	7
Total	100

Types of car crime

The term 'car theft' covers various patterns of offending typically categorised in the literature (Clarke, 1991) into six types:

1) theft **from** vehicles;

2) theft **of** vehicles for so called 'joyriding';

3) for use in the commission of other crimes (eg, ramraiding or getaway cars);

4) for immediate transport;

5) for longer term transport;

6) as part of insurance frauds.

These types of offending will often overlap—a 'joyrider' may steal from a car he has taken and offenders may progress from one type of car crime to another.

3

Nevertheless, it is necessary in considering policy options to recognise the distinct categories of crime involved. As will be seen, the study addresses the categories above to varying degrees.

Offender studies

Two types of offender studies are already available, the first of which are self-report studies of offending. These provide detailed information on some aspects of car crime, but generally suffer from small sample size, single geographical location and, in some cases, a less than rigorous methodology. Secondly, there are semi-structured offender interviews. Two domestic studies are available (Briggs, 1991; Spencer, forthcoming) though both use a relatively small sample size drawn from a single research site.

Offender studies have concentrated on young offenders who have usually been apprehended—an easier sample to locate than those who have not been caught. They mostly focus on the where, why and how of car crime and many have come up with similar findings. Five of the most interesting have been carried out in Sunderland, Greater Manchester, Northumbria (two) and Northern Ireland.

The Sunderland study (Spencer, forthcoming) was conducted in 1990 under the Safer Cities initiative. Of particular interest is its use of a general sample of young people, rather than the more usual offender-based group. The sample— 86 boys aged 10 to 16—was made up of schoolchildren from the Pennywell Estate and surrounding area—areas with much higher than average rates of car crime, extremely high unemployment, and severely overcrowded housing conditions. The study took the form of a self-report questionnaire. Among the findings were that 52 per cent knew someone who had stolen a car or stolen from a car; 80 per cent thought boys did it for the money; 80 per cent thought it was a group activity; of those involved, 45 per cent did so with older boys; and the main target was fast cars that are easily stripped. When asked what they thought could be done to stop boys getting involved with car crime, only about half responded, and most said that more activities for young people would help.

Spencer also held a car crime discussion group at a youth club with nine young people, as well as interviews with 17 car offenders (aged 13–19 years) selected through the probation service. The data collected reflected other findings on the car crime process, but also looked at motivations and the social backgrounds of offenders. Early motivation was said to be primarily to 'experience driving', but this changed as offenders got older and more experienced—when money took over as the primary motive. One thief had been expelled from school, and seven said that they could not see the point of going to school. Better leisure facilities were said to be a possible way of preventing them from becoming involved in car crime.

The Manchester study (Smyth, 1990), using a sample of 86 car crime offenders (most aged 18–21), formed part of a joint police/probation car crime campaign and was therefore fairly crime prevention orientated. Among the findings were that 74 per cent took Fords and Vauxhalls; 52 per cent said they would be put off by an alarm and a further 40 per cent by an 'Autolok'. The main reasons given for taking cars were excitement (58%), financial gain (47%), and liking driving (43%). A majority of the sample (72%) said that they always took cars with their mates and when inside a car the radio/cassette player was the first thing they would attempt to steal (77%). The sample was not very specific about the places they took cars from, but backstreets and car parks seemed to be targeted most.

The first Northumbria-based research was a probation-led study of 56 young 'car crime specialists' referred to the probation service for social inquiry reports (Gulliver, 1991). The results are broadly similar to the Manchester study. An attempt was made to categorise offender types by motivation into 'professionals', 'marginals' and 'obsessionals'—not dissimilar to the offender hierarchy noted by Briggs (below).

The second Northumbria study was that of Briggs (1991) who interviewed 30 convicted TWOC offenders aged 11–17 years to provide a 'profile of the juvenile joyrider'. Several common social factors were identified—disrupted family backgrounds; unemployment; poverty; below average academic ability; abbreviated school careers; and socially deprived inner-city residence. Similar backgrounds apply to the majority of those apprehended for juvenile offending and as such are not surprising. More interesting is the meaning ascribed to 'joyriding' by those interviewed. Briggs found evidence of a hierarchy of activities which carried correspondingly increased kudos for the participants, the higher they progressed up the ladder, and the more publicity their exploits received in the media. This gave rise to expressions of pride in and boasting about the activities in which members of the sample engaged. Further, Briggs suggested that 'skilled' operators would act as teachers and role models for other less adept or 'amateur' participants.

The Northern Ireland report was produced by the Extern Organisation (McCullough *et al.*, 1990). It contains results from two statistical studies (relating to South Belfast and Northern Ireland) and an interview study of offenders and professionals working in West Belfast. While much of the Extern data coincides with that produced by mainland research, the particular political situation obtaining in West Belfast makes cross-over comparisons difficult. Having said that, the discussion of policy implications from the study makes for interesting reading and many of the findings are worth considering.

Structure of the report

Chapter 2 presents the criminal biography and social background of the sample. Chapter 3 examines the car crime career—how it starts, develops and stops. Chapter 4 considers results of particular relevance to crime prevention—where, when and what vehicles are vulnerable, and car security. Chapter 5 discusses the criminal law response and the effectiveness of sanctions as a deterrent to car theft. The results of the study are reviewed in Chapter 6, and their main policy implications identified.

2 Offender profile

This chapter presents findings on the extent of the sample's involvement in car crime and other offending, as well as data on their home, school, work and leisure backgrounds.

Car crime biography

Age first involved

Almost half the sample (47%) said that they were 14 or 15 years old when they first started taking cars. Figure 2.1 shows that one person began at the age of 10, while at the other extreme, another did not start until the age of 25.

Sixty-eight per cent said they got involved with car crime while still of school age—although not all were still attending school (see below). Of those who had reached school leaving age when starting to steal cars, most (66%) were unemployed. For the sample as a whole, only two per cent were working when they started to steal cars; 22 per cent were unemployed.

Up to the age of 15 slightly fewer had driven on the road than had begun car crime, suggesting that after becoming involved, it took a little time before stolen cars were actually driven (see Chapter 3). Figure 2.2 presents details of when respondents had first driven, whether or not this was in connection with stealing a car.

Slightly tangentially, the current sample's opinion on when others started to commit car crime produced an average age of 14, though answers ranged through nine (n = 3) to 19 (n = 1). This reflects the typical age of their own involvement.

Length of involvement

In all, 28 per cent of the sample had less than 12 months car theft experience, 46 per cent had been involved for at least two years, and 21 per cent for more than five (six of these having offended for more than 10 years). Not surprisingly, age was linked to length of involvement in car crime (Figure 2.3).

The vast majority of the 15/16 year olds (n = 21) had been involved in theft for between six months and two years, whereas for the 18–20 year olds (n = 24),

7

Figure 2.1
Age first involved in car crime

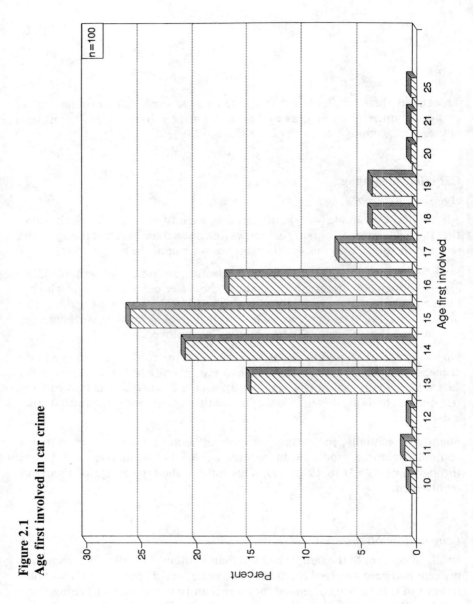

Figure 2.2
Age subjects first drove on the road

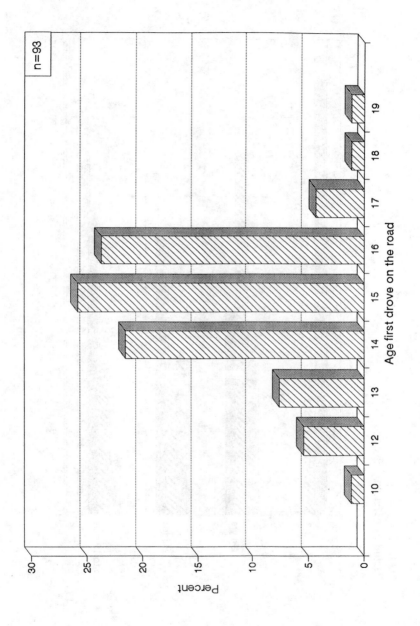

9

Figure 2.3
Period of offending, by age

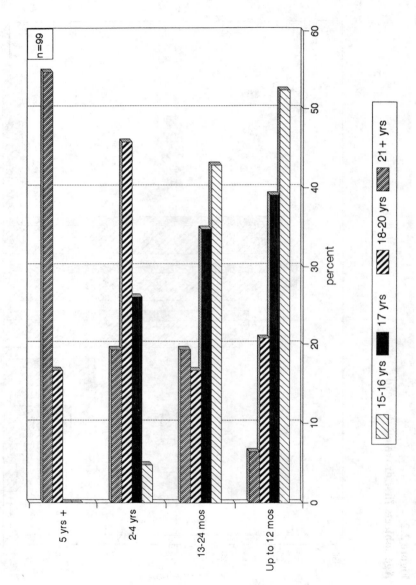

nearly two-thirds had been involved for at least two and a half years, and over half had been involved for four years or more. Among 21–25 year olds (n = 24), nearly six out of ten had been involved for four years or more.

Number of offences

Interviewee accounts of the number of cars they had stolen may doubtless be prone to error and exaggeration, but taken at face value, just under half of 15–16 year olds reported having stolen over 100 cars. For the 17 year olds, a third reported having stolen between 11 and 50 cars and the largest group (36%) reported having stolen several hundred. A core of relatively inexperienced thieves were among the 18–20 year olds in the sample: 9 out of the 24 had stolen between 1 and 10 cars. However, ten of the 18–20 year olds said they had stolen at least 100 cars and five several hundred. About half of the 21–25 year olds also reported stealing several hundred cars. Five of the seven subjects older than 25 reported stealing several hundred cars over their career.

Table 2.1 presents the facts as reported by interviewees. Extrapolating for these figures suggests an estimated 7,000 cars stolen by the 100 thieves interviewed, the average number of cars stolen was about 45 for those under 18, and 94 for those older.

Table 2.1
Number of cars stolen (n = 98)

	n
1–5	13
6–10	6
11–30	11
31–50	10
51–100	13
101–200	7
201–300	4
301–400	1
500 +	33
Total	98

Frequency of offending

Three-quarters of the sample said that at their most active they committed offences at least two or three times a week (Figure 2.4). While the estimates given of the number of cars stolen over their full careers (see above) may have appeared high, they would by no means be impossible to achieve given these stated weekly levels of offending—assuming that these too were not exaggerated. A large proportion of respondents from the North of England (84%) fell into the three highest categories for frequency of offending.

Figure 2.4
Frequency of offending (peak of career)

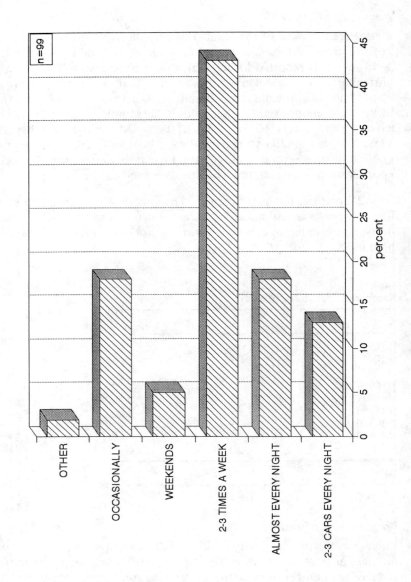

Contact with the police

Twenty-one per cent of the sample had never come to police notice—15 of them under 18 years old. Twenty-five had been caught once, and 15 twice; fourteen had come to police attention more than eight times. The chance of having been caught increased with age; few older offenders had escaped the attention of the police altogether. All told, four out of five of the sample had been caught by the police at least once, though given the nature of the sampling this is little guide to 'true' apprehension risks.

Still offending?

At the time of interview, 60 per cent of the sample (n = 97) said that they were not now involved in car crime, though it is uncertain, of course, how many of these were giving a 'desirable' answer—and in any event two-thirds of the desisters had given up only in the last few weeks. Twenty subjects (21%) said they had desisted for six months or more—fairly evenly spread throughout the 15 to 25 year age group. Six of the 18 desisters aged 21–25 years had stopped for more than two years. Desistence is considered further in Chapter 3.

Experience of other crime

The extent to which car crime offenders form a discrete group specialising in car crime or also engage in other types of crime is considered in Chapter 3. Suffice it to note here that many of the sample had been involved in other crimes including burglary (35%), ramraiding (20%) and 'other thefts' (11%).

Social background

A number of recent studies of car crime acknowledge the importance of looking at the social background of offenders. For example, McCullough and Schmidt (1990), describe the historical and political context of car crime in West Belfast and suggest that structural and long lasting problems such as unemployment cannot be ignored. Spencer (forthcoming) identifies inadequate schooling, unemployment and poor leisure facilities on the Pennywell estate in Sunderland as contributing factors, and Briggs (1991) also draws on the theme of social deprivation, highlighting problems of inadequate opportunities for excitement and status. The present research was designed to explore three particular aspects of offenders' social background—home, school/work and leisure. It should be noted, as pointed out in Chapter 1, that as the sample mostly came from the lower socio-economic groups the data presented here reflects that bias.

Home

Most of the sample (76%) were living with parents or in homes of their own at the time of the interview; six per cent were currently living in children's homes and nine per cent were in hostels. Not surprisingly, most of those aged 19 or under (70%) lived with one or both parents; 44 per cent lived with both parents and usually siblings, and 26 per cent lived with one parent and, in most cases, siblings. Of those over 19, under a third remained with parents. Thirty-seven percent had moved on to live with partners (30% having children also) and most of the rest lived alone or with friends.

Although over three-quarters of the sample (76%) said that people at home knew about them taking cars, many added that the family knew only of the times when they had been caught and had no idea of the full extent of their involvement in car crime. Those who said that people at home did not know about them taking cars (19%) often mentioned being afraid of their parents finding out—several people said that they thought their parents would 'kill' them should they ever find out. More than three-quarters (78%) of those whose families were ignorant of what was happening were from homes where no one else was said to be involved in car crime, and almost half (42%) were aged 15 to 16 years. Older offenders were more likely to have families who knew about their activities—presumably because their repeated offending inevitably came to light eventually.

Of those who said that people at home knew about their offending, 59 per cent said that they were angry and upset—and indeed for a few people getting into trouble at home had been enough to stop them taking cars (see Chapter 3). Of those whose families were very bothered something under half acknowledged that they were powerless to do much:

> They didn't like it at all. They said there's nothing they could do but they stuck by me when I was doing it and going to court.

> They used to nag me a bit till I was about 18, but now they know they can't stop me.

> They hate it, they don't like it at all, they shout at me but they don't actually ground me—if you're going to ground someone you're just going to make them more angry inside.

> If they start giving you a hard time for it, you just rebel and go out and do it more.

> They'd turn round and say 'If you take another one we're going to tell the police'. They were trying to talk me out of it and get me to do other things but they obviously saw it wasn't going to stop me because I was getting a buzz out of nicking cars.

The ultimate sanction—that they had been kicked out of home—was reported by 12 per cent of the sample. Some said that their car crime activities had escalated after being excluded from the family home:

> My mother kicked me out once and I went berserk—started pinching cars more and more.

> My parents lost all respect for me. They told me they didn't want me at home any more. I was homeless on my 16th birthday. I can see they did it for my own good now.

14

Only 11 per cent of the sample said that people at home were not or would not be bothered about them taking cars. Some of these were simply told to take responsibility for themselves:

> They don't react any more because they say 'it's your life, do what you want with it'. I think that's fair enough because it stops them worrying.

> My old man said 'At least you didn't get caught for it—I can't really give you a hard time because I used to do it'.

In some of these cases, people at home had expressed the view that they did not want to know anything at all about the offending and merely advised offenders not to get caught and to be careful to avoid having an accident.

Family involvement in car crime

A third (33%) of the sample said that others in the family, usually a brother or cousin, also took cars or had done so in the past. One person said that he had been pressurised into stealing by his father who was an experienced car thief. Yet even those with others already involved in car crime said that their family was or would be angry and upset about their own involvement (34%). Several older people said that if their own children started taking cars they would be very hard on them:

> I'd give him hell. My advice would be 'Touch a car—steal another car and I'll break your arm'. Maybe that's a bit rough but it's fun to steal a car if you're that age and be able to drive around with your mates . . . I would stamp on it if it was my son, because I've actually been there, I know what it's like.

In summary, then, two-thirds of the sample were living with one or two parents when interviewed. In three-quarters of cases, people at home knew about their involvement in car crime, and one in three interviewees had other family members involved in similar offences. Family members were less likely to know what was going on when the family was criminally uninvolved, or when offenders were relatively young. When families did know, most felt angry, upset or unhappy about it. Relatively few (12%) excluded the offender from home. There was little evidence that families were indifferent to the offending or uninterested in stopping it. However, if the offender chose to ignore the family view it appears that there was little that parents felt able to do about it. Some families clearly felt their hands were tied by their responsibilities as primary carers and protectors—responsibilities which might be seen at odds with throwing the offender out of the home, bringing in the police, or instituting care proceedings.

School and work

Although no questions were asked specifically about experiences at school, several people said they regularly took time off school in order to take and drive cars:

> It's usually arranged the night before. Someone rings up and says 'Do you want to go for a ride?' I say 'See you all tomorrow morning' and I knock off school for the day.

As found in the Sunderland study (Spencer, forthcoming) many people said they did not see the point of going to school and some had been expelled:

> It was just boring, I really didn't like it. Once I had a week off and I got caught but it still don't bother me. My Nan used to say 'you know you've got to go to school' but she couldn't really make us go. We just used to go out and sit in the park or stay in the house watching telly.

School was also mentioned as a place where car parts might be bought and sold.

Of those who had left school officially or unofficially (n = 94) a few (3) said they had stopped attending school as early as 12, most (63) did so between the ages of 14 and 16. Only three stayed on at school until they were 17 or 18. At the time of the interview most of the sample were no longer at school and over half of them were unemployed, albeit some attached to motor projects (Table 2.2).

Table 2.2
Current occupation (n = 100)

	%
At School	6
Employed	6
Unemployed	49
Motor Project	10
Special Needs courses	10
Youth/Employment Training	16
Other	3

Not surprisingly, unemployment was frequently mentioned as a major problem:

> There's nothing to do round here for young people—no jobs. Everyone's bored and skint.

> It's pretty horrible because there's no work here, there's no work anywhere else and I don't think we're going to come out of the recession as quickly as everyone reckons.

> Nothing to get up for. No job in the morning. No money at the end of the week. You know you have to find some way of getting money and nicking cars was usually the easiest way.

However, some acknowledged that employment would not necessarily stop people earning money by stealing cars:

If you've got a job, you've got money and you go out and buy whatever you want. You spend the money then you want more, so you got to go and get more off a car, then you steal another car for more wheels.

In contrast, others suggested that having a steady job would be one of the main things that would stop people taking cars:

If they're in work, they give it up—it's all money.

Whilst training schemes were seen as a way of gaining qualifications, some people said they could not afford to live on the allowance:

You're seventeen years old, you get put into training for a good job and you're there for a year. You're nearly as good as a trained bloke—you get about £35 a week when he's taking home £130. What can you do nowadays for £35? Fair enough, you're learning a trade, but I still think you should be given a bit more money.

When asked for their career aspirations, over a third of the sample (35%) mentioned car-related occupations. The question may of course mean rather different things to a young teenager than to someone already in their 20s, but Table 2.3 nonetheless gives the results.

Table 2.3
Employment aspirations (n = 92)

	%
Didn't think about it	20
Motor mechanic	16
Something to do with cars	11
Rally driver	8
Army/Navy	6
Other professional sports	5
Police force	3
Bricklayer	3
Professional artist	3
Medicine	3
Fire service	2
Chef	2
Carpenter/decorator	2
Other	16

Despite the preference for car-related occupations, 20% lacked any employment aspiration at all, and there was little difference between younger and older thieves in this respect. Some said they deliberately avoided thinking about the future:

At school when they were talking about careers and all that, I used to hate it. I always used to think of myself as a failure for not getting anywhere. The future used to frighten me—even talking about it.

Lack of job opportunities, low wages, inadequate training allowances and benefits are problems which may make criminal activity financially attractive—more attractive anyway than doing nothing and just hanging around at home or in the streets. While boredom, unemployment and lack of cash may be common experiences for many teenagers, for the present sample they were seen as an inevitable part of the future too. They were not optimistic about the prospect of finding work and legitimate opportunities to earn money.

Leisure

For a number of people leisure activities depended on whether or not they had money to spare. Table 2.4 reflects this in showing the activities people said they usually engaged in when not at school, working or stealing cars. The most common response, especially for the under 18's, was hanging around, for which little money is needed.

Table 2.4
Typical leisure activities (n = 95)

	%
Hanging around/sleeping	39
Driving or working on cars	8
Sport	8
Music/drawing	8
Other crime	8
Watching TV/videos	3
Visiting girlfriend	3
Taking drugs	3
Going to pub	2
Gardening	2
Other	16

Sport was seen by some of the sample as a legal alternative to taking cars:

> I play football and go on a Sports Leadership course . . . I can't really play football. I'm alright but its just something to do . . . I've been jet skiing and got quite a buzz out of that and I've been in speed boats with a couple of my friends. It's a good laugh, you know you're not breaking the law. You can have a real good laugh . . . I always try to find something to do but it isn't easy. In the winter it's worse.

A number of things were done to reduce boredom. Some said they would normally sleep during the day, others said they would go to amusement arcades, or into a park to sit and talk to people. For some, when they were bored, taking cars 'for the hell of it' was one way of having fun—a point returned to in Chapter 3.

Some said that they would feel particularly bored at night:

> I was doing a lot of football, judo and karate, but after 10 o'clock at night, I would start getting bored. I wasn't drinking then—I was only 16, just hanging around with nothing much to do.

> The first time we did it, we were bored. We were just sitting in the house at four o'clock in the morning and none of us could get to sleep so he said to me 'What can we do cos we're bored?' and I said we could do that [steal a car] if you want. Two of the boys didn't want to do it, then two more said 'Come on, let's do it for a laugh'. So we all went out and did it for a laugh.

Lack of facilities for young people was often mentioned as a major problem:

> I was bored there wasn't anything else to do in the area. The nightclubs and discos and things like that were either for the over 21s, or they were boring.

> There's nowt to do where I come from, nothing to do at all. They say go to the youth club and that, but what's there to do over there?—play tennis with idiots.

> All it would take would be for them to give us somewhere where we could loaf, that doesn't close at 11 o'clock . . . Somewhere we can hang around where we could all go and keep warm and do what we want to do in peace . . . I mean we've got television and youth clubs but we're always all around at one or two o'clock in the morning and there's no harm in us being around. If the police don't like it they should give us somewhere we could go.

Table 2.5 shows what the sample said they liked doing best, when not working, at school or taking cars. As can be seen, sport figures more highly than car-related activities, but almost a quarter of the sample (23%) reported having no favourite activity.

Table 2.5
Favourite leisure activities (n = 89)

	%
None	23
Active Sport	29
Mechanics/driving	11
Getting drunk/out of it	9
Music	8
Watching TV	3
Going to clubs/raves	2
Other	15

When asked what they would choose to do if they could do anything at all, almost half the sample (48%) mentioned car-related activities, rally driving

19

Table 2.6
Ideal activity (n = 94)

	%
Rally driver	13
Something to do with cars	12
Mechanics	10
Sport	10
Other manual job	8
Long distance lorry driver	5
Drive legally	4
Travel/go on holiday	4
Having lots of money	4
Social work	4
Other	18
Don't know	8

being the most popular. Those who mentioned social work often said they wanted to work specifically with people on motor projects (Table 2.6). Sports ranged from football and fishing to adventure sports, deep sea diving and flying. There are clearly differences in responses to this question, with some answering about ideal jobs, others about their general aspirations.

It is perhaps hardly surprising, given the prevalence of car-related activities (48%) and the desire for excitement, that some people described taking and driving stolen cars as a dangerous sport in its own right, requiring courage, dexterity and practice:

> It takes a lot of time to learn how to do these things. To display a car well isn't just going up and down the road handbraking. A lot of the small kids think it should go backwards and forwards handbraking—it isn't that at all. There are a lot of other manoeuvres like a reverse flip where you steam backwards down the road and you flip the car round and put it into first before the car's finished moving. It takes a lot of practice and co-ordination.

Summary

Most of the sample became involved in car crime in their mid-teens, and thought others did so too—rather older than suggested by more imbalanced recent press coverage. The sample generally claimed an extensive career in terms both of length of involvement with car crime and number of offences committed. Four-fifths had been in contact with the police, although it seemed clear that many had escaped police attention for much of their offending. Six out of ten claimed to have given up car crime, but only 20 claimed to have desisted for more than six months. Many of the sample had committed offences other than car theft.

Parents appear concerned about their children's involvement in car crime. Some attempt to prevent it happening; others appear powerless to stop it. For most of the sample school appeared to them of little value. Career aspirations were low or non-existent and unemployment high, with little prospect of finding work in the immediate future.

Despite the abundance of spare time, leisure activities were severely restricted by lack of money and the inadequacies (perceived or real) of local facilities— which offenders themselves linked to their criminal activities. Time hung heavily on their hands, and seemed likely to do so in the future.

The social background of the offenders in the survey mirrors that of young offenders generally. Many strong illustrations were provided of the hopelessness of growing up in a lower working class environment, and frequently offered a perspective in which delinquency was an obvious repsonse to limited social and economic opportunity. This accords with the view of McCullough *et al.*, (1990) that for those who have no identity conferred by work or education and no real hope for the future, existence is grim and car crime becomes an exciting option.

3 The car crime career

This chapter looks at three stages in the career of the car thief: first, the circumstances surrounding initial involvement; secondly, how the career develops; and thirdly, issues concerning giving up car crime.

Initial involvement in car crime

With whom did car thieves first become involved?

Nine out of ten of the sample said that they first became involved with peers, usually having one to three companions with them on their first few experiences of car theft. In the Newcastle sample, all subjects began in the company of others. Eight out of ten of the sample said that peer behaviour was a very important factor in their initial involvement: it was felt unlikely that they would have begun on their own—'no I don't think I would have got into car crime unless other kids were involved'. This said, a small minority (n = 4) felt it was important that they were on their own when they first tried to steal a car, mostly for reasons of safety and to reduce the risk of being 'grassed on' to the police.

Acquisition of skills

A third of the thieves said they were taught the basic skills of car theft—breaking in and starting the car—by friends of the same age, usually people from the local neighbourhood. A fifth were taught by older 'mates', and a similar number by a mixture of older and same age friends. Regardless of their age, the vast majority of associates were more experienced than members of the sample at their initial involvement: only six claimed that their associates were as inexperienced as they were:

> You get into groups of five, seven . . . you all go out and walk the streets. You've got a bunch of keys, sledgehammer or whatever. There's normally about two who don't know what they're doing. There's always one who knows how to drive, knows how to get into it, knows how to disarm alarms—you just stay around, bide your time and just listen. You go on a few jobs and then you turn around and think 'yeah, I could do that', then I'll get my mate and go off.

Driving skills came about somewhat differently. As with breaking in and starting the car, the more experienced drivers were willing to teach other offenders. Four out of ten were taught by mates, but the same number claimed to have taught themselves by trial and error having watched others drive. (Practice was usually off the road.) Fifteen per cent said that they had been taught by a member of their family, usually a parent, before they became involved in crime.

Eight subjects could not drive at all at the time of the interview, and a further two could drive, but so badly that they did not drive on the road. The non-driving cases were spread evenly throughout the 15 to 20 age group—less concentrated amongst the very young respondents than might be expected. As seen in Chapter 2, many subjects felt confident enough to drive on the road as early as age 14.

Apprenticeship

In line with research done in Belfast (McCullough *et al.*, 1990), early careers often involved a learning period which did not necessarily involve driving itself. Initiates tended to be the 'lookout' while mates did the breaking in and driving. The novice role seemed not to last for long however: the subjects in this study seemed soon to become part of a team in which roles were swopped quite frequently:

> I always used to be his passenger . . . and then one day he said to me you have a drive. Then one day I stole a car and he was the passenger. I'd say it took me about eight months before I did it myself.

> It felt cushy when we (first) used to go . . . well my mates used to go up . . . they used to drive . . . I used to sit in the back, four in the back two in the front. Then we would take turns . . . It would be someone's turn (to break in) on Monday, someone's on Tuesday.

Motives surrounding initial offending

Interviewees were asked what they thought was the main reason for their first getting involved. Peer influence (31%), boredom (18%) and the search for excitement (18%) were most frequently mentioned as primary reasons (Figure 3.1).

The 'main reason' question, intended to elicit spontaneous answers, was followed by a list of other possible reasons—based on findings from other research with car crime offenders—which subjects were asked to rate on a scale of one to four: unimportant, quite important, important, very important.

Responses to the prompted explanations for becoming involved are shown in Figure 3.2. Seventy-one per cent of the offenders rated potential excitement as important or very important; 66 per cent rated 'being bored' similarly; and 58 per cent 'just drifted in' to car crime. Asked about other people entering car theft, the interviewees also felt that they were typically also those with nothing to do (31%)—or stupid or immature (16%). (The question was asked in the context of whether 'joyriding' was becoming more popular where they lived: somewhat disconcertingly, incidentally, 71 per cent of the sample felt it was.)

23

Figure 3.1
Main reasons for initial involvement

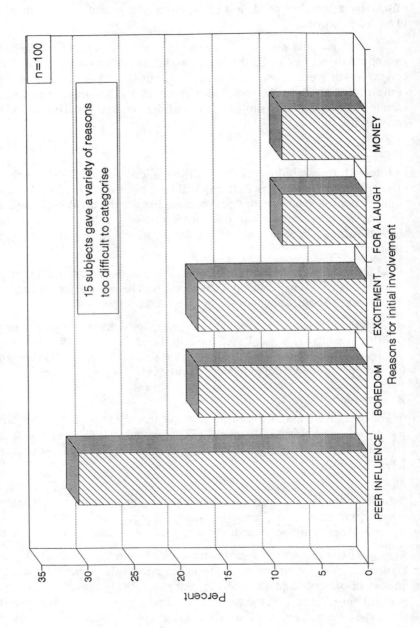

Figure 3.2
Further reasons for initial involvement

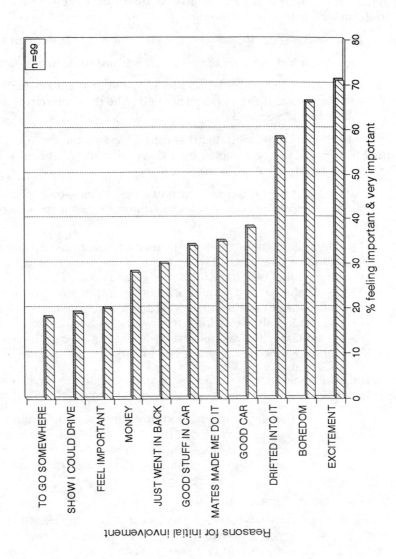

Peer influence

As seen, nearly a third of offenders cited 'peer influence' as their main reason for getting involved in car crime, though it was clear that this denoted more of a gradual and subtle 'drifting in' process than direct pressure from peers to conform with offending behaviour:

> Because everyone else was doing it . . . you just followed suite.

> Most of the kids were car thieves . . . it was just something I started doing.

> I did it to be one of the boys. You see all your friends doing it and they come home and they tell you all about it. And then you start thinking 'well shall I go and get one?'

A third (33%) of those who said that others were important also stressed the need to impress and be accepted by a group of mates as the most important reason for getting involved in the first place:

> All my mates my age were getting into it same as me—only to be up with the boys. In a way you're driving so you think you're a man—it seems you're grown up.

> I wouldn't have got involved on my own because I was so insecure— I just wanted to be liked. I used to do anything for my mates really, whatever they were doing, whatever they were getting up to, I'd get up to as well. That's what everybody wants when they are young—to be liked. The brainboxes of this world and the kids that get on with their work just aren't liked. I think really deep down there was only one or two of us that was really into taking the car, the rest of us was just doing it because we were just following the crowd, you know like following the leader.

Several people said that it was the companionship of mates which made up for the instability caused by parents breaking up:

> I wasn't getting any response from my parents at all because they were going through their own problems . . . the only input I was getting was from my friends. I went along and sort of wanted to see how important I could feel because of what I was doing when I was with them.

Boredom and excitement

Although the search for fun and excitement is, of course, characteristic of young people, Chapter 2 showed that boredom was a major problem for those without money and jobs and that taking cars was often seen by many of the sample as a way of 'curing' boredom. This view is further supported by findings from a recent survey of a thousand 16–25 year olds on 'young people and crime' (NOP, 1991). In the present study, for some it was the prospect of driving that made taking cars so exciting:

> It was just for the buzz—the enjoyment of driving.

> Since I was about 14 I wanted to get in cars and drive . . . it's not worth going out and nicking a car unless you enjoy driving or something.

For others, the excitement lay in fear:

> The first time I was really nervous and shaking like a leaf all the way through but as soon as I'd parked the car up, I went 'Yeah! Great! I can't wait to do it again'.

Some people described taking cars as more than a cure for boredom—as an adventure in its own right, a chance to go away, for instance:

> We wouldn't stay around here, we'd go to a seaside town—go on the beach and go swimming.

> We'd tour all round the country, go from place to place running them out of petrol, getting another one and carrying on.

Passion for cars

How far a heightened degree of interest in cars might be a spur to car crime was considered by asking subjects when they had first become interested in cars and whether or not this was linked with the onset of their offending. Just over a third of the sample did not report any particular early interest in cars: their current interest seemed more exclusively linked with criminal activity. But some two-thirds—across a span of age and car crime experience—said that they had a keen interest in cars from an early age:

> I used to go to Brands Hatch with me Dad and I said hello to James Hunt. I've been addicted to cars since I was a right little kid, but I've never had the opportunity to have my own car and that's the only thing I ever really did ever want.

> I was driving tractors when I was nine and then one day he asked me to move his car and it was totally different. It was a smoother engine, it went faster and I thought 'Wow, I could like this'. He used to let me take it up and down the lane when I was about 11 and I used to give it hell. In them days I used to have to get behind a wheel and if I couldn't get people to lend me their car, I'd go and nick one.

The vast majority who reported a pre-offending interest in cars rejected the idea that this was particularly implicated in the onset of their criminal behaviour—though there was a hint of a regional difference in that 12 of the 29 Newcastle subjects (41%) felt their previous interest in cars was linked to their eventual offending.

To sum up, first experiences of car crime were overwhelmingly in the presence of other more experienced peers and for many peer influence was very important in their initial involvement. It is difficult to say whether peer influence is more important for car thieves than for other 'apprentice' offenders, though clearly the present sample relied greatly on others in learning the skills of the trade. There is some evidence that the novice is given more minor roles, such as lookout, and may well not drive immediately. Overall, the indications are that generally recognised adolescent experiences such as being bored, wanting to be one of the group, and needing excitement, are primary motivating factors in initial involvement in car crime. Factors such as wanting to feel important, wanting to show off driving skills, having a means of transport, and—interestingly—a way of making money, were quite far down the list.

Previous studies have not focused as specifically on the area of initial involvement as the present one, but their findings have not been dissimilar. Briggs (1991) in Newcastle, Foster (1990) in South East London, McCullough and Schmidt (1990) in Belfast, and Smyth (1990) in Manchester have noted the importance of peer group acceptance and the search for excitement as central to involvement in car crime. These studies also noted the rather bleak existence of many young car thieves.

Career progression

When interviewed, the current sample of thieves had generally had an extensive career in car crime and had been very active at the peak of their careers—a large proportion claiming to have been involved in the theft of several hundred cars (Chapter 2). How had their career progressed from its early stages, and did they persist in car crime for the same reasons they had started?

Eighty-three interviewees answered questions about how, if at all, their activities had changed since they first got involved in car crime. While six, who had been offending for a relatively short time (6 to 12 months), said there had been no change, for the others it was apparent that as careers progressed skills improved, and incentives and motivations in relation to car crime shifted. A changing role for peers was also apparent.

Changes in skills

A third of the sample (most having offended for at least a year; and three-quarters of them aged 18 to 24) said that they had become more skilled in the process of stealing cars, in terms of technique and speed:

> When I first started it didn't matter how I'd do it—I'd break a window if I had to get in. I'd rip the dash to pieces. Then I learnt there's a lot easier way to do it . . . through the locks with a screwdriver.

> I can do it faster. I can do it better. I still go to the same places. It takes me eight seconds to get into a car.

> I used to put the window in, now I use screwdrivers.

> Back then, we used to smash a quarterlight using a scaffy bar . . . but now I like do the door locks with a screwdriver and rip the alarms off . . . use a

28

wrench. One time if there was an alarm I used to leave it, now it's no problem.

An improvement in driving skills was also claimed by many, though previous studies (Briggs, 1991; Gow & Peggrem, 1991; McCullough *et al.*, 1990) emphasised the tendency of offenders to overestimate their driving skills and to have little knowledge of the Highway Code.

The role of the peer group

As noted earlier, the role of peers began as teachers and rapidly progressed to that of co-offender—who were now needed as lookouts, for moral support and to increase enjoyment. An elementary division of labour was apparent:

> You need at least three people to go out . . . like someone's behind you. If I was black boxing[1] it or scaffing it, somebody's behind my back in case someone tried to jump on me. There'd be two people at one end of the street and one at the other end just keeping toot.

> We probably all knew different things . . . one was a better driver, one was better at getting in, one knew the area better.

> It's a bit scary on your own. It's like if you are with someone, you know you are both doing it together—I mean you don't want to get caught on your own.

A small minority of the sample (9%) said it was important that they worked on their own usually because it was seen as reducing the risk of being caught.

Ten per cent of the sample said that they progressed to selling cars to receivers for profit, and this issue—progression to what could be termed 'professional' car theft—is dealt with below.

Incentives to car crime

The interviews underlined the fact that car crime careers continue for a number of reasons, which can be termed either 'expressive' or 'instrumental'. The former encompasses car crime engaged in for the thrill of it, for status, etc; the latter refers to car crime with a further purpose in mind—financial gain, through selling cars or their parts—which if developed sufficiently, may be termed 'professional' car crime. The two categories should not be seen as discrete and offenders may commit offences from either or both motivations. Nevertheless, this classification is useful when considering whether incentives to car crime change with age and experience, particularly in relation to the types of offending behaviour considered here: 'joyriding'; performance driving; theft from cars; progression to 'professional' theft; and ramraiding.

---

[1] 'Black boxing' consisted of removing the plastic casing around the steering column, followed by the ignition/steering lock, to expose the starter motor switch (or black box).

'Joyriding'

The term 'joyriding' (which first appeared around the turn of the century, originally meaning a pleasure trip in a car or plane), has taken firm hold in relation to car theft—despite criticism that it undermines the misery caused to its victims. From offenders' accounts here it is clear that an element of 'stealing for kicks' underpinned many incidents of theft—indeed being a necessary if not always sufficient condition for it:

> The best thing about the whole experience is speeding about.

> It gets more exciting once you're in the car—once I'm over 60 I'm off . . . I go a bit mad sometimes when I'm driving. I just wouldn't take things easy when I was in a car, I'd always have to say 'let's go A to B, the fastest way there' . . . the bigger the car the bigger the power trip you get.

It is difficult to estimate figures on either the proportion of incidents committed principally for 'joyriding' purposes, or the proportion of offenders who would have labelled themselves 'joyriders'. An indicator, however, is that over a third (39%) of the sample reported abandoning a car within a few hours, or by the next day (21%).[1]

Performance driving

Performance driving—or 'frisking' as it is termed in the North East—consists of driving a car to its limits (and beyond) in terms of road holding, braking, speed and manoeuvrability.[2] As well as usual driving skills, use is often made of some motor sport techniques, the most common being to spin the car through an angle of 180 degrees so that it ends up facing and can be driven off in, the opposite direction.[3] Doing this can, of course, be highly dangerous, especially if committed on the roads by inexperienced and highly excited drivers. An added dimension, which turns performance driving into display driving is when such manoeuvres are performed in front of spectators—as highlighted by the media in the summer of 1991.

A majority of the sample (58%) said that they enjoyed performance driving, though this was rarely the sole purpose for stealing cars. (A further three offenders said they had engaged in this sort of driving, but not on public roads).

---

[1] A further 7%, incidentally, said they usually 'torched' the car after use, and, while this is not itself evidence that the initial purpose of theft was joyriding, it does preclude the use of the car itself for profit-making activities (aside from insurance frauds). Twenty per cent kept the car for a few days, and only 10% for a few weeks, as regular transport. (All those who kept cars for a long period were 17 or older.)

[2] The term 'hotting' was coined by the media in the summer of 1991, but was unfamiliar to most of the offenders here.

[3] This is achieved if the car is being driven forward by pulling up hard on the handbrake (a 'handbrake turn') which causes the rear of the car to slew round, the car being driven off in the direction from which it came. If the car is travelling in reverse, a technique referred to as a 'reverse wheel flip' is used in order to spin the car through 180 degrees (as this technique is rather less well known it is probably unwise to detail it here).

'Performance drivers' tended to be younger, with 54 per cent being 17 or under (as opposed to 33 per cent of those not into performance driving). In fact, a substantial number of those not interested in performance driving were older, as Table 3.1 shows.

Table 3.1
Experience of 'performance driving', by age (n = 100)

Age	Performance Driver	Not Performance Driver
	%	%
14	2	—
15–16	21	20
17	31	13
18–20	24	26
21–25	17	31
26 +	5	10
	100	100

It was clear, however, that performance driving was a rewarding element of theft for many:

> Handbrake turns, reverse turns, screeching the wheels . . . if I'd a fast enough car I'd race it about a mile until the bizzies (police) come and you get chased.

Many of those who said that they wanted to impress their mates often held competitions and races to see who had the most powerful car and to test their driving skills against each other:

> If I had a car and someone else had a car, you'd race and see which machine was the best and spin around. It's showing your friends what you can do with the handbrakes.

The degree to which the 'buzz' and 'thrill' contributes to car theft makes this form of crime distinctive, and this will be returned to when dealing with motives below.

Theft from cars

As careers progressed the number of offenders who stole items from or off cars increased to more than nine in ten respondents (92%), a finding very much in line with other studies. By far the most popular items to be taken were radio/cassette players (mentioned by 63 of the 97 subjects asked the question). A further 17 per cent said that as well as radio/cassette players they would take anything lying around in the car or boot—coats, bags, tools:

> Sometimes I don't believe what people leave in their car like—they leave bags, sports bags, brand new coats, coats in the back seat and that . . . brand new leathers and handbags and that sitting in the back of a car.

Stealing from cars was an activity that ran parallel to stealing cars themselves. Seventy-six per cent of subjects said that they had broken into cars merely to steal items without intending to steal the car itself. Of these, nearly half did it regularly, and for the duration of their car theft career; only 22 per cent said they had done this occasionally. Eleven subjects said that their involvement in car crime had started with theft from cars.

While a great number of incidents resulted in driving the car away, the financial rewards of stealing from the stolen cars was obviously seen as an essential perk by at least a third of the sample. Some even saw it as an essential source of income:

> I'm not working and my social at the moment's been stopped. Normally, I go out once a week and do a stereo run and I'll nick about 40–50 stereos in a night. They're all to order—I don't nick cheapies anymore.

'Professional' car crime

A tenth of the sample mentioned specifically that a feature of their career development was that they went on to selling cars for profit—one of the activities conventionally seen as a component of 'professional' car crime (Clarke, 1991). Selling cars or their parts for profit also arose in connection with questions about the destiny of cars once they had been stolen. Thirty-five per cent of the sample (n = 98) reported that having taken a car they used it for 'professional' theft activities. (It was clear that many of these engaged in more than one of the following activities, but stated their preferred one.) Most often this involved taking the car to a garage to strip it and sell the parts (n = 15), or taking it to a receiver (n = 10). Six subjects mentioned 'ringing' the car—changing its identity using false number plates and documents and selling it on. Four subjects mentioned experience of doing 'insurance jobs'—ie, destroying a car so that the owner could claim from an insurance policy.

Though nine out of ten of the sample made money from car theft by selling radio/cassette players and items found in the car, the third of 'professionals' (as they shall be termed hereon) represent a departure in terms of career and motivation to activities more obviously linked with organised financial gain. The following quotes illustrate the range of their activities:

> I look for wheels, smart interior, things like that because I strip the cars I do, and sell the parts.

> I've learnt through the years that I can make a lot of money out of cars. Say you asked me for an RS Turbo and you wanted the engine, interior, bonnet, back hatch and wheels. I'd say £1000. You couldn't buy it for that, it would cost you six.

First of all it was for 'joyriding' and impressing friends and then it progressed up to stealing cars for the money . . . people wanting cars to sell on . . . I used to phone someone up and he used to tell me what car he would want, what colour, year, make . . . so I'd go out and steal a car like an XR3 which is nippy, will stick to the road and could be handled very easily, so if I did get a chase I could get away. And then I'd look for Cosworths, turbos, Mercedes, BMWs, those sorts of cars . . . sometimes they were going abroad.

I change all the number plates and sell it as a new car. I'd buy a knackered out Mark 2 Escort for £30 so I've got the documents, then I go and nick a tidy Escort but with the number plates and aluminium plates cut out of the chassis of the old car. I take it up to a car auction and I sell it.

Though age and experience were implicated in theft for profit to some degree, they had less influence than might be expected. Half those who mentioned stripping cars for parts were relatively young, at 16 to 18 years old. Similarly, those who had been involved in 'ringing' cars were evenly distributed between ages 16 and 22. One of the respondents doing 'insurance jobs' was 16. The single activity where age and experience appeared more strongly implicated was selling the car to a receiver. Those involved were mostly aged between 18 and 25, and eight out of the 10 had been involved in theft for four years or more. Numbers are small for definite conclusions, but there is a suggestion within subjects' reports that a reputation as a good car thief had to be achieved before being approached by a receiver to steal to order:

. . . through the people you know and meeting other people, it progresses from 'I know someone who wants those wheels' to 'I know someone who wants the whole car'.

I'm just starting to get into the serious part of pinching cars now like ringing them up by myself and that . . . This bloke just came up to us, I knew him anyway, and says can you pinch us an XR2 and I'll give you £150. I said no problems and I asked him what he was doing like and he explained everything, how to get plates everything . . . I still pinch odd ones just to frisk about in for a bit of fun.

Ramraiding

Using a stolen car to smash into and steal from commercial premises is a difficult activity to locate on the professional/non-professional continuum. Whilst one aim of ramraiding is unquestionably to make money, the stolen car is not itself the source of profit, but rather a means to it, albeit lending a strong element of excitement to the escapade as well:

I love doing it . . . I would do the driving in the van. We'd take two cars like six people, three in one, three in the other. I would drive up, drive in the shutters, pull out . . . four people running in the shop filling the cars up. Like we'd time each other—three minutes, in and out in three minutes. I like the noise of the alarm bells ringing . . . it's good.

Twenty subjects chose to define themselves as ramraiders, and eight had engaged in other professional activities as well (two stripped cars, two ringed cars, four sold to receivers). As might be expected, they were also more experienced: 13 out of 20 having been involved for at least four years. From subjects' accounts, it appeared that the concept of ramraiding embraced both organised money making and thrill to some degree, but either way it seems linked to progression in the car crime career. If ramraiding is classified as a 'professional' thieving activity and added to the other profit-making activities described by subjects, a total of 47 per cent of the whole sample could be seen as having engaged in professional car crime.[1]

There was some evidence that ramraiding was more common in the North of England sample, but numbers were too small to draw firm claims.

Changing motives in career progression

While the main incentives to begin stealing cars were seen to be the example of peers, boredom and potential excitement, it is clear that the motivational underpinnings become more complex as the theft career progresses. Typically, after about a year, skills seem to have improved sufficiently to allow thieves to steal better cars, and with greater speed. For many (45), these improved skills are harnessed to increase the thrill of theft. But for at least a third of thieves, they are also a means of turning theft into financial gain. In other words, while expressive needs are still part of the equation, there is a shift in balance towards instrumental needs.

The distinction between taking cars for the thrill of driving and taking them primarily to earn money is reflected in the fact those who do it for money were often highly critical of joyriders:

> They realise they're twats. I mean what they're doing up in Birmingham and Manchester . . . it's stupid looking for police chases. It's making it harder for people like me who make a living out of it.

> A lot of people take cars just to drive around to joyride but they don't think positive like where are they going to get some money from.

This picture is supported by answers to a specific question on the main reason for persisting in car crime. Figure 3.3 looks at the motives of those who had at least one year's experience in car crime, the point around which competence appeared to improve.

Clearly, for many (42%), money has now overtaken 'the buzz' and having 'nothing else to do' as the main feature of continued involvement in car crime.

---

[1] Eight out of 20 ramraiders, as said, were already included in other professional categories (which they were more likely to engage in than ramraiding). They are, of course, counted only once.

Figure 3.3
Main reason for persisting in car crime

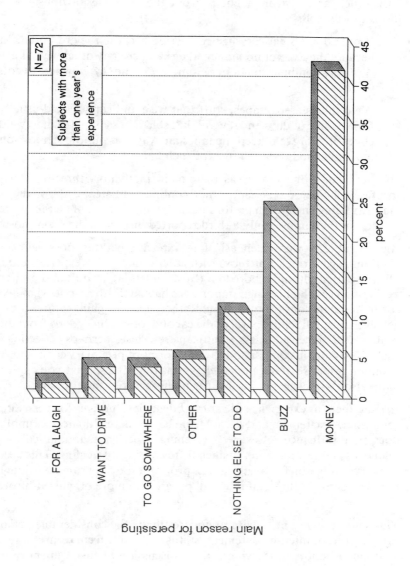

Interestingly though, of those citing money, only about half had become involved in 'professional' car crime. The money to be made on a more casual basis, such as by stealing goods from the car, was obviously a powerful motivator as well:

> People don't steal cars just to joyride because they're bored, they steal because they've got no money, they can't see any other way of getting out . . . It's a combination of boredom, loss of money, nowhere to go, nothing to do.

> We'd take stereos, tapes, stuff that we could carry. We'd usually keep it for a couple of days and if we hadn't sold it in a couple of days we'd usually chuck it. But we'd keep the tapes anyway and put the stereos somewhere until somebody wanted one for their car.

Of those not citing money as their main motivator, three-quarters had no 'professional' theft experience; they continued to steal cars for the buzz, the majority being engaged in performance driving. In fact, of all the 'performance drivers' in the sample, only a third reported money as the main motivator.

Again, subjects were then asked to rate another ten possible reasons for continuing car crime. For those with at least one year's experience, Figure 3.4 illustrates that although boredom ('just something to do') and excitement are again rated very highly, their importance had diminished somewhat in comparison to initial reasons for offending. Rather, material gain features prominently, achieved through selling parts of the car and/or stealing goods from the car. To 'sell the car' received a less significant response, perhaps reflecting its more exclusive nature in comparison to other forms of pecuniary car crime. The most common response of all, nonetheless, was that 'It's so easy you can't resist the temptation'—a clear pointer for car manufacturers and owners.

In sum, then, as experience of car theft develops, motives for persisting change somewhat. Excitement and release from boredom remain heavily implicated, as does peer influence. However, widening experience undoubtedly opens up many possibilities for being financially rewarding by stealing. This becomes the primary motivator for a substantial proportion of the sample, though it does not necessarily ensure that they will progress to more organised 'professional' car crime.

This said, it would be unwise to underestimate the considerable personal pay-offs in terms of intense excitement, status and self-esteem recurrent throughout subjects' accounts of thieving cars. A discussion of this element of car crime and the somewhat compulsive behaviour it fuels follows.

The role of compulsion in car crime

Studies on burglary (Nee and Taylor, 1988b; Bennett and Wright, 1984) and shoplifting (Carroll and Weaver, 1986) have strongly suggested that target selection in these crimes tends to be less of an opportunistic whim, than the

Figure 3.4
Further reasons for continuing

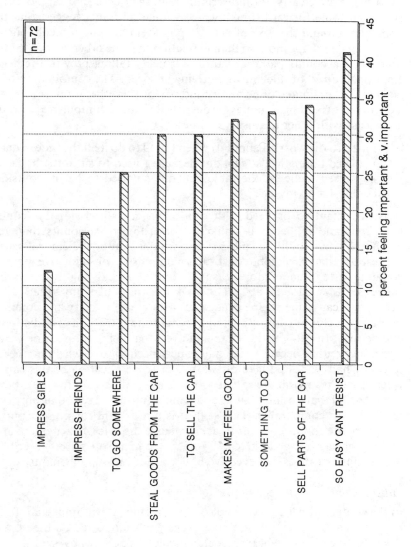

result of a more rational series of decisions to offend, beginning away from the scene of the crime, and ending as a response to learned cues at the crime site about the likelihood of success (see Cornish and Clarke, 1986, for a more detailed discussion of the 'rational criminal').

Car thieves are clearly not indiscriminate in their choice of targets either, and engage in some forward thinking. Also, their accounts suggest that plentiful opportunities and the ease of acting upon them are undoubtedly big spurs to offending—perhaps more so than in relation to some other crimes. At the same time, their accounts paint a picture of quickly falling prey to the heightened emotional 'buzz' of thieving and driving at speed. The combination of what is perceived as unlimited opportunity and personal gratification, seems to lead to a degree of offending that may be described as more compulsive in nature than is the case with other acquisitive crimes:

> I used to (be worried about it) when I used to do it all the time. That's when I started taking Ma's (car) out because I used to sit in the house and the keys used to be on the table and the car used to be just outside and I couldn't stop myself.

It is important to proceed with caution in any discussion of 'compulsive' behaviour and crime. It is unlikely from subjects' accounts that any were exhibiting what could be called a true compulsion in the clinical sense. (The suggestion that car theft constitutes compulsive or addictive behaviour is certainly often made more casually than any existing research evidence suggests.) McCullough *et al* (1990) noted that, like any other adolescent behaviour, car crime can be engaged in with great 'ferocity and commitment', but saw it as closer to any other adolescent infatuation than to addiction. Forty-one per cent (n = 94) of the sample did feel that being 'hooked on' cars was a possibility, either because they had experienced an overwhelming need themselves or had witnessed it in others.[1] A further indication of this came about when asked if anything else felt as good as stealing cars (n = 69). Forty-four subjects said that nothing felt as good and a further 12 said that only the effect of drugs was comparable. This said, it is not helpful for present purposes to 'diagnose the condition', but to acknowledge the role of excitement and other 'psychological' rewards in car crime in comparison to other crimes. The implications of this for preventive policy are addressed in Chapter 6.

Substance misuse and car theft

In the context of heightened emotion in car crime, it was important to find out to what extent, if any, alcohol and drugs were implicated on the occasions of theft. Fifty-eight per cent (spread equally across age groups) said that they did not use drugs or alcohol in connection with car theft. About a third of the

---

[1] There was no relationship here with substance misuse—about half of those who felt it was possible to become 'hooked on' cars used drugs, half did not.

RADZINOWICZ
LIBRARY
INSTITUTE OF
CRIMINOLOGY
CAMBRIDGE

sample (32%) regularly used drugs (14% in combination with alcohol), most commonly before stealing the car and then continuing while driving around. Unfortunately, there are no figures regarding drug use among the general population with which to compare these figures, but, in any event, they suggest a potentially treacherous combination of inexperienced driving, impaired ability, and increased confidence. Only six respondents claimed to use alcohol alone before and during stealing cars, though this figure should be treated with caution given that an estimated six per cent of 'normal' males aged 17–24 drive while over the legal limit on a regular basis (Goddard, 1991).

One in ten of the sample admitted to using cannabis on its own when they were stealing cars, and a rather larger proportion (14%) to combinations of cannabis alcohol and glue. Drug and alcohol was common across all age groups, though cannabis use was most concentrated amongst the 15–20 year olds. Those from the Midlands (15 out of 21) were less likely and those from the South-West (10 out of 22) slightly more likely to use drugs and alcohol in conjunction with car crime. Though questions about general drug use were not asked, four subjects mentioned that they did use drugs, but not in connection with stealing cars:

> (I'd use) not very strong stuff, just cannabis. A lot of my mates take acid and would be driving around while they're tripping, but I was too scared of the drug.

Experience of other crime

An issue of particular interest in relation to career progress is whether or not the present sample of thieves specialised in car crime, or were involved in a mixture of other offences. Thirty-two subjects had no experience of other crime. The rest, including those who now specialised in car crime (see next section), had mostly committed a mixture of crimes, the most common being burglary (n = 35), or ramraiding (n = 20—though 11 ramraiders had done nothing else but car theft). Eleven subjects had committed other thefts, mostly comprising of shoplifting and a further 11 were not specific about their other crimes. On occasions, a car was stolen for other purposes, particularly by more experienced offenders. Nearly half the sample admitted to having stolen a vehicle to commit other offences, most often burglary.

Car crime specialists?

Respondents (n = 97) were asked if they had specialised in car crime to the exclusion of other crimes and just over half (n = 53) said that they had. This is not to say that specialists denied other offending entirely—though 10 of the 53 made mention only of ramraiding (arguably simply a developed form of car crime—which is certainly how most of the ramraiders saw it). Apart from ramraiding, only a quarter (n = 13) of the specialists admitted to having experimented with other crime, usually burglary. Nearly all of this group said they experimented after their car crime career had begun, though car theft was more attractive to them and they had reverted to it:

I tried other things like burglaries, theft from shops, commercial burglaries and I never really got into it. I couldn't get to grips with the way to do it. With cars it was so easy. You'd just walk up to it, put a screwdriver in the lock, unlock it, put a scaffold bar in the ignition, whack it off, black box it . . . the car's started and you're off. With things like burglaries there's more to watch out for. If the house or shop is alarmed, you have to cut the alarm and they're more difficult than on cars.

There was no strong evidence that those with experience of 'performance driving' were more likely to be specialists, or that specialists engaged more in 'professional' theft—with the exception of those who worked for receivers who were more likely to be specialists.

However, some distinctive features of those who defined themselves as specialists emerged. First, they had longer than average experience (Figure 3.5). For instance, 25 per cent had a career span of at least five years, whereas this was the case for only 15 per cent of those who were 'into' burglary (n = 26), and two out of 11 of 'other thieves'. Secondly, specialists were more likely to begin their criminal career with car theft (92% had done so, as against 42% of others). Thirdly, while specialists did not begin to offend any earlier than others, they drove illegally on the road earlier: 40 per cent had done so by the age of 14 (the youngest at 10), as against 28 per cent of non-specialists (the youngest at 12). Fourthly, and perhaps most importantly, specialists appeared to offend more often. For instance, 61 per cent said they stole cars at least two or three times a week—much higher than among non-specialists (37%). The greater criminal activity of specialists is no doubt a factor in stronger parental reaction to their offending. A full 63 per cent of specialists said their parents felt angry or upset by their thieving, in contrast to 37 per cent of non-specialists.

Specialisation appears to have roots in an unusual degree of interest in cars before thieving starts. (Sixty per cent of those who ended up as specialists had a childhood interest in cars, as against 37 per cent of non-specialists.) This early interest was reflected in their job aspirations when younger: 40 per cent of specialists aspired to some car-related occupation—be it motor mechanic, rally driver or simply 'something to do with cars'—as against 18 per cent of non-specialists. This early interest in cars maintained itself too: 59 per cent of the specialists most wanted to be currently engaged in a car-related activity, a higher figure than for others (41%).

In sum, then, just over half the sample considered themselves to be car crime specialists, concentrating more or less exclusively on stealing cars. They were more likely to have been interested in cars from an early age and aspired more strongly to (legal) car-related jobs when young. They were much more likely to have begun their offending career with car crime, and to have sustained a more active career, offending for longer and more often.

To what extent might the degree of specialism in this group of offenders be unusual? Several studies have looked at the degree to which offenders

Figure 3.5
Length of involvement: specialists and non-specialists

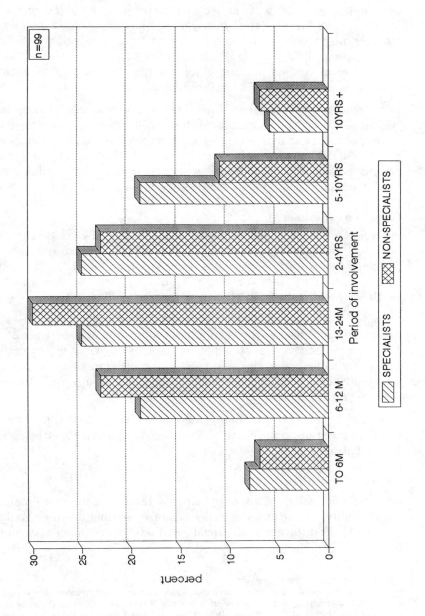

(particularly juveniles) specialise or not in a particular crime (eg, Farrington *et al.*, 1988; Klein, 1984; West and Farrington, 1977). All comment on the great degree of offence versatility, though Farrington *et al.* (1988), using sophisticated statistical methods of analysis to study the juvenile court careers of 70,000 offenders aged 7 to 17 in the United States, found that vehicle theft was one of the three most specialist offences. In an early British study of borstal boys aged 16–20 between 1953 and 1955, Gibbens (1957) too, found over a third of car thieves had more than one conviction for the offence, and commented that 'such recidivism is probably very unusual'.

In a recent review of research, Tarling (1991) also concludes that there is some evidence of specialisation among car thieves, albeit weak.[1] The present research differs, of course, in that thieves were asked to define themselves as specialist or not, and the sample size is much smaller than in other studies. Nonetheless, the present research is in line with other work in suggesting that stealing cars may be a more specialist activity than many other crimes.

Giving up car crime

Subjects were asked if they or any of their friends had given up car crime, for how long, and why; whether or not they thought car crime was becoming more popular; what sort of person was attracted to it; and why they thought people gave up car crime as they grew older. Those still offending were asked whether anything would realistically stop them from offending.

As noted in Chapter 2, 21 per cent of the sample could be seen as genuine desisters having given up for six months or more (half aged between 21 and 25). A further 39 per cent were potential desisters, having given up for a few weeks. Those that had not given up, and those that claimed to have given up recently, were more heavily concentrated in the younger age groups, with three-quarters aged 20 years or under.

Sixteen subjects, who had not given up themselves, said that they had friends who had given up, and five of those who had stopped had friends who had stopped also.

Reasons for desistence

Of those who had given up, over half gave reasons of increased maturity and responsibility, from simply growing out of it, settling down or getting a job (n = 19), to the influence of girlfriends/partners, or becoming a parent (n = 13).

---

[1] Three British studies, for instance, have used 'transition matrices' to calculate the probability of an offender committing the same type of offence in a series of offending (Stander *et al.*, 1989; Home Office Statistical Department, 1985; Phillpotts and Lancucki, 1979). The results depend heavily on the categories of crime deployed. 'Unauthorised theft of a motor vehicle' was treated separately in only one study (Home Office Statistical Department, 1985) and even then it was subsumed under 'Motoring Offences'.

Three subjects said that the distress caused at home by their car crime was enough to make them stop:

> My mum just started going wild, she would freak out on me—couldn't handle it any more so I just stopped.

> My girlfriend would get distressed and call me childish, it's not worth upsetting her.

Only 13 subjects said that the threat of prison had finally deterred them, with a further subject desisting after having served a custodial sentence. Five subjects said that having an accident made them desist, though four of these had only recently given up and all were aged 17 or under. Two said that attending a motor project had enabled them to give up. Table 3.2 summarises reasons for stopping.

Table 3.2
Reasons for giving up car crime (n = 58)

	n
Threat of prison	13
Did time	1
Remand in custody	1
Grew out of it	10
Girlfriend	10
Settled down	7
New baby	3
Got a job	2
Accident	5
Motor project	2
Other crime	1
Other	3

There was no difference in reasons given for desisting between those recently giving up and the longer-term desisters. Nor did the car crime 'specialists' have any distinctive reasons. When asked why they thought other car thieves might give it up when older (n = 84), the reasons given were similar to the maturity/responsibility responses above, in particular: 'grow out of it' (36%), 'just settle down' (20%) and 'more to lose' (8%). One in ten said that people do not give up when older.

Finally, 34 of the 39 subjects who continued in car crime were asked if they felt there was anything that would realistically make them desist. Five mentioned the threat of prison, five said that having money would help, and five took the stance that nothing would deter them. However, the most singular feature was the diversity of answers from others (with a few—but only a few) mentioning being able to drive legally, attending a motor project and having a job. The lack

43

of any particular factor that would have influenced a sizeable proportion of offenders out of car crime argues against there being any easy remedies likely to have far-reaching impact.

Deterrent effect of road accidents

Over three-quarters of the sample (78%) said that they or their friends had been involved in accidents and only 10 per cent had no experience of accidents at all (n = 84). For almost a third of the sample (32%), accidents had resulted in serious injury and a further 18 per cent (n = 14) had experienced a friend dying. (For three subjects a friend dying in an accident was the worst part of their car crime career.) The number reporting fatalities seems remarkably high for a sample of 100 but may be explained by the fact that nine of these subjects were from Newcastle and were probably referring to a small number of fatalities known to them all.

Twenty-one per cent of the sample (n = 98) said the worst part of their car crime experience was having had an accident, and for seven it was the risk of having one. But this was often seen as an unavoidable part of the danger of high speed driving, rather than as a deterrent. Only five interviewees said that having an accident had made them desist, though a third admitted to an accident putting them off for a few weeks. Despite a possible degree of bravado in their responses, this indicates a characteristically high degree of motivation and determination (*cf.* McCullough *et al.*, 1990), if not youthful feelings of immortality, a belief that 'it will never happen to me', and a high degree of confidence (perhaps misplaced) in driving ability:

> As they say, if you fall off a horse, just get straight back on—don't be scared, because if you don't get back on you're going to be scared for the rest of your life.

> As soon as I was out of hospital, the first thing I did was to steal a car to make sure I could still do it.

Those that claimed not to be deterred by accidents at all were older and more experienced; there was some consistency to these claims, in that they reported a considerable number of serious accidents during their careers.

To round up, then, 21 per cent of this sample had desisted from car crime for a considerable length of time. Thirty-nine per cent reported giving up recently and 40 per cent continued in car crime. Those that had desisted tended to be older. The desisters said they had given up because of increasing responsibility and maturity and these reasons were also given by others when asked why they thought people might give up when older (in line with McCullough *et al.*, 1990). When asked directly why they had given up, less than a quarter cited the threat of prison as their main reason. The experience of serious accidents and fatalities did little to deter the car thief either.

Summary

The majority of car thieves in this sample began thieving at age 14 or 15 in the company of other more experienced car thieves. They quickly became competent, in terms of technique and speed of execution, after a period of apprenticeship which appears to end at around six to twelve months. Having begun because they were bored, their friends were doing it, and it was obviously thrilling, the possibility of financial reward from theft—either on a casual basis (including theft from cars) or on a more organised one—quickly became apparent. Consequently, while the thrill remained important, for many making money became a strong factor in continuing. At least one third engaged in what have been termed 'professional' activities; and nearly half of the sample were ramraiders or professionals. Increased age and experience were implicated to some degree in all types of professional crime, particularly with stealing cars to order for a receiver, and ramraiding; but it is worth noting that stripping and ringing cars, and destroying cars for insurance purposes, began as early as age 16.

An unusual degree of 'psychological' reward in terms of thrill, status and self-esteem was highlighted, and may be implicated in the excessive rate of offending. This may be particularly the case in those not dominantly motivated by money-making—often the less experienced car thieves and 'performance drivers'.

Those who had desisted gave greater weight to reasons of increased maturity and responsibility for giving up than the effect of penal sanctions. This, in turn, may be related to the fact that a major factor in beginning and continuing car theft is the need for excitement—rather typical of the age group but likely to weaken with maturity. This was also true of the wider sample when they gave reasons why other people might give up car crime.

A large group of self-professed car crime 'specialists' was identified (53%) who claimed to focus more or less exclusively on car theft. They were characterised by a particular passion for cars from an early age; longer experience of car theft; and more frequent car thieving expeditions resulting in more numerous thefts.

Several issues have emerged in relation to the progression of the car crime career which have implications for diversion and prevention. These include: the virtually unlimited opportunity for car theft according to subjects' accounts; the short but consistently stated period of 'apprenticeship' and what this might mean for intervention; the apparent opportunities for progression to 'professional' car theft at a relatively young age; the unusual degree of emotional pay-off from theft and the way in which this may negatively affect the offender's perception of traditional penal sanctions; and the identification of a large group of car crime 'specialists' who, if they are typical of the wider population, may be effectively targeted to prevent a considerable amount of car theft. These and other issues are discussed in Chapter 6.

4 Crime prevention issues

This chapter brings together results which have implications for 'physical' crime prevention. The information is presented under two headings: (i) the vulnerability of cars to theft in terms of where and when they are parked, and make and model; and (ii) vehicle security.

Vulnerability to car crime

An accurate indication of the vulnerability of cars parked in different places at different times would need to take into account the total number of cars parked at various locations and how this varies by night and day. Without these baseline figures, the offenders' accounts reported here (and indeed the findings of most other studies) can only be suggestive as regards where and when cars are at greatest risk.

Location

This said, previous research has identified residential kerbside parking and public car parks as the most common sites for car crime and this was largely supported by the present study.[1] Gulliver (1991) and McCullough *et al.* (1990) suggest residential kerbsides may present higher risks, whereas the present study identified public car parks as a preferred car crime site for 37 per cent of the sample, with residential kerb side parking mentioned by only six per cent. However, a large proportion of respondents did not specify where they took cars from—28 per cent taking cars from 'anywhere' and a further 18 per cent from 'somewhere quiet':

> We just take them from different places like, we used to go to the hospital or somewhere like that and take them from the big car parks, that sort of thing, or down the car park in town, by the quayside.

Car parks were identified by Briggs (1991) as high risk (53%) and in a self-report study of offenders in South Wales, 66 per cent cited car parks as favoured crime sites (Gow & Peggrem, 1991). Spencer (forthcoming) found too that 'the majority felt that car parks anywhere were likely targets'.

---

[1] For a recent analysis of car crime in public car parks, see Webb *et al*, 1992.

Timing

Forty per cent of offenders operated after dark, with only eight per cent saying that they operated exclusively in the daytime. The remaining 52 per cent said they operated at any time. Those that operated after dark were mostly unoccupied during the day, suggesting that they chose darkness to reduce visibility. This was, indeed, evident in many of their accounts. Other studies, however, report a higher proportion of offenders who limit their activities to after dark (though Spencer (forthcoming) and Smyth (1990) are exceptions). The lower level of night-time offences here may be partly explained by the large number in the sample who took vehicles from car parks:

> If it were dark we'd take it from anywhere . . . if it were daytime we'd take 'em from car parks.

Of those who favoured car parks as a location 69 per cent operated 'at any time' but 80 per cent of those who targeted vehicles parked outside houses did so only after dark:

> I'd do it in the daytime but you wouldn't go outside people's houses in the daytime—not unless it was alright. If it had the keys in it you'd just jump in, you wouldn't try and break in outside their house in the daytime.

Perhaps the most significant finding is that almost half of the offenders (47%) did not restrict their offending to either times of day or to particular locations.

Type and make of vehicle

A sizeable minority of this sample were also indiscriminate about which cars they stole. When asked whether there was anything about a particular vehicle that would put them off taking it, 29 per cent of the sample replied no. Of those who said there was, 12 per cent (mostly aged under 18 years) mentioned factors such as unpopular makes and for one interviewee:

> Sometimes colours and things like that—if it's not a very good colour—I wouldn't drive about in a pink car or something like that.

Most significantly, 49 per cent (spread over all age groups) responded that they would be put off taking a car if it was fitted with an alarm. The full range of responses can be seen from Table 4.1.

The Home Office *Car Theft Index* (Houghton, 1992) presents the risk of illegal taking and theft of (but not from) fifty volume-produced type of cars, adjusted for the relative numbers on the street. (The *Index* is based on offences recorded in England and Wales in 1989–90.) Fords and Vauxhalls dominate the high and medium risk groups, while the likeliest cars to be stolen come from a small category of usually older models—Capris, Cortinas, Escorts, Fiestas, Metros and Astras. Cars from this category, it was estimated, may be at up to four times greater risk of theft than other cars. Higher performance cars, it was suggested, were up to three times as likely to be stolen as lower performance

Table 4.1
'What would put you taking off a particular vehicle?'
(n = 94)

	%
Nothing	29
Alarms	49
Unpopular make	10
Know owner	2
Age of vehicle	2
Disabled badge	2
Location	1
Other	5
Total	100

cars, with some models as much as 10 times as likely to be stolen. As will be seen, offender responses in this study matched well with the data contained in the *Index*.

Similar to other studies, cars most often targeted by the current sample were 'easy to steal' (32%) and 'fast/performance cars' (36%). Others said they first took cars which were easy to steal, then, as they gained experience, moved on to high performance cars (17%):

> At first it was just easy targets—Cortinas with sloppy locks and things. Then it moved on to getting just what I wanted—anything I felt like driving.

When asked which vehicle makes/models they were most attracted to, 43 per cent replied Fords, 15 per cent Vauxhalls and 10 per cent mentioned both—a combined total of 68 per cent:

> I look for sporty types like XR2s, RS Turbos, two litre Cortinas, Escorts. I just walk around the streets at night.

That easy cars are targeted is not surprising; nor that fast/performance cars are wanted, much as they are by a large proportion of the young male population generally. The success of the car manufactures, media and advertising agencies in turning fast cars into objects of desire clearly affects not just potential customers, but also those who are barred from legitimate access to cars either for economic reasons or because they are below the legal age for driving.

Why do Fords and Vauxhalls feature so prominently in this and other studies even when the figures are adjusted to take account of the large numbers on the road? Part of the answer seems to be that they are considered particularly easy to steal:

> I just look for cars that are easy to nick—cars that aren't alarmed, general stuff like Fords and MGs and Austins that are easy to get into. Nissans,

Toyotas—mainly Japanese makes like Subaru are really hard to get into because they've got awkward locks.

As well as ease of theft, however, it may be that offenders have more knowledge of and feel more confident around makes such as Ford and Vauxhall, which could be even more disproportionate in numbers in their rather poor home environments than on the road generally. Other makes—for example for continental and Japanese manufacturers—are likely to be under-represented, which may reduce offender's confidence in their ability to enter and start them.[1] This view is reinforced by the fact that after Fords and Vauxhalls, Austin/ Morris cars were mentioned as easiest and most popular to steal. The prominence of particular models in less affluent locations has significance for the calculations contained in the *Index*, since although adjustments were made for the over-representation of Fords and Vauxhalls on the road, this was a global rather than area-based calculation.

Data from the *Car Theft Index* shows too that older makes—also likely to be over represented in the offender's home environment—are particularly vulnerable to car crime.

In sum, then, three types of car seem particularly at risk: first, older cars which may be easier to steal; secondly, familiar cars, with which offenders feel comfortable; and thirdly, performance/sporty cars which offenders would like to own if given the opportunity.

Crime prevention issues

Vehicle security: locks

Methods of car theft matched those found in other studies. For this sample, the most common method of getting into cars was to force the door lock, using a screwdriver (53%) or keys (18%), (keys being more likely to be used by older offenders). Others were not specific about their technique for gaining entry (24%). Only two per cent said that they broke a window to get into a car—most presumably avoiding this because of the noise and the visible signal given to others, including the police, that the car had been stolen. Those who had were in the younger (15–17) age groups, reflecting their lack of expertise.

Many offenders expressed incredulity at the ease with which locks could be picked or forced using any key or a screwdriver:

Ford. Always a Ford—they are just so easy. The locks normally fall apart, there's nothing to them.

The first car I nicked was a Vauxhall Viva, I opened it with my garage key, which surprised me.

---

[1] For despite the view offered above, it seems that locks on other, for example Japanese, makes are not objectively 'more awkward'.

> Fords—the easiest cars of the lot to pinch, it's unbelievably easy. You can guarantee you can get into it.

By far the most common method of overcoming the ignition/steering lock—described by 66 per cent of thieves—entailed breaking away the plastic trim around the steering column to expose the ignition barrel which would then be shattered or snapped, mostly using a short piece of scaffold tubing, the diameter of which allows it to be slid over the standard ignition barrel (often referred to as 'scaffing'). The ignition/steering lock could then be removed and the exposed starter motor switch ('the black box') operated.

Again, many offenders remarked on the ease with which this could be achieved:

> Astras (are easy) 'cos like the steering lock's easy and the case. Just rip the case off, there's a black box at the back of the barrel, hit that open, turn it round with a screwdriver, starts up straight away.

> Fords are always easier because the ignition barrels just come off a piece of piss.

Vehicle security: alarms

Results from previous studies on the deterrent value of alarms are both limited and mixed. Questions were framed here to provide information on perceptions of alarm systems, the relative effectiveness of different types, displacement effects, and experience with alarms.

Not surprisingly, given the large number of alarm systems on the market, roughly half the sample seemed confused and ill-informed regarding makes and types. The other half of the sample however displayed a sound knowledge, together with some quite ingenious methods for disabling alarms—information, which for obvious reasons, will not be detailed here.

When pressed on the subject of alarms, 34 per cent said that all alarms deterred them; 18 per cent said it depended on the make of alarm, and nine per cent the model. This suggests that depending on makes and models, alarms might deter as many as six out of ten of the offenders interviewed. This is significantly less than Briggs (1991) who reported that 83 per cent of his sample said they would be deterred by an alarm, but matches the Manchester findings (Smyth, 1991). In the Newport study, 50 per cent of the sample reported being put off by alarms (Gow & Peggrem, 1991).

How did offenders know that a vehicle was alarmed? Although some mentioned window stickers, a much larger number said that they would look for a flashing red light (LED—light emitting diode) on the dashboard. This raises the possibility that just a light and/or sticker alone might be a useful deterrent. While this may be the case for some offenders, others were clearly aware of this:

> Sometimes they're just flashing lights, they are not proper alarms, just a deterrent. And when they've got stickers on and there's no sign of an

alarm, if you want to take the car you've just got to try it because sometimes they're just blank stickers.

Many said that they would kick a tyre or do something similar to check whether an alarm was fitted and in use. If the alarm sounded they would just stroll away—some would return to attempt to take the vehicle; others would try another car.

The limited response indicated that 33 per cent of thieves considered all alarms to be easy and 40 per cent mentioned one particular make of alarm as being readily overcome. As to easy types of alarms too few responded to give reliable data—reflecting a lack of knowledge of the systems or an inability to describe them properly. But of those who did respond, 64 per cent mentioned remote control and 18 per cent door activated systems as being easy. A similarly inadequate response was given when asked which alarm types and makes were difficult to disable.

Nine per cent reported that they had never triggered an alarm during entry to a vehicle. Of those who had, 54 per cent said that they deactivated the system, while 37 per cent reported leaving the vehicle and running away. (In the Manchester study, 64 per cent said they would run away if they activated an alarm (Smyth, 1990).) Of those who had deactivated an alarm, the most common methods cited were to crawl under the front of the car, reach up and detach the wiring from the alarm, horn or battery, or to 'pop the bonnet and pull the wires out'; if this did not work 'just smash the alarm with a hammer'.

The ability to deactivate alarms increased with confidence and experience:

> When I was just starting things like alarms would put you off but you learn things all the time . . . how to get around alarms.

A surprisingly high proportion of those claiming to have deactivated an alarm were in the youngest (15–16) age group, which one might expect to be least skilled. This may suggest an element of exaggeration in their claims. It would have been interesting to put them to the test, and ask them to demonstrate their methods.

On the question of whether thieves felt that people took any notice of alarms 'going off', 12 per cent said yes, 46 per cent replied no and 39 per cent answered sometimes. In the Manchester study a lower figure of 30 per cent felt that an activated alarm would probably be ignored.

One interviewee made the point that:

> They take more notice of people running than the alarm itself, say you've gone in and popped the bonnet, the alarm's going off now, just get out of the car and stroll round the front, they think its yours, your having trouble with your alarm. The only person you've got to worry about is the geezer actually walking back himself.

Even among those who claimed that alarms could be defeated or were in any case ineffective, many would prefer not to take an alarmed vehicle:

> I prefer to take a car without an alarm because it's less hassle, just jump in and drive away.

> I wouldn't bother with it if it had an alarm on it I'd just go and look for one that had no alarm, less hassle really.

> Car alarms can put me off, they're quite effective. Certainly, if me and me mates were walking around and we'd seen a car with an alarm on we'd leave it just for the sheer aggravation of having to deal with it.

But for the more determined offender:

> If there was a good enough car you'd take it. If it had an alarm you'd disconnect the alarm.

In sum, while the findings indicate that alarm systems can be an effective deterrent, more information is needed about the relative efficiency of types and makes. The ability of offenders to deactivate alarms also needs to be further tested.

Theft of audio-equipment

The interviewees offered some comment on one of the two systems recently developed to protect audio equipment: 'pull outs'—radio/cassette players which are slid out of the dashboard and taken from the car. Many of the offenders found that owners often do not bother to remove the radio-cassette, especially when leaving the car for short periods, else they leave it under the seats or in the boot of the car. Thus, some broke into cars even though the cassette player was not in its casing, expecting, often correctly, that it was hidden in the car. One described doing 'stereo runs'—targeting residential streets around 5pm to 7pm when 'people haven't bothered to take out their stereos and are having their tea'.

Vehicle Watch

In Vehicle Watch initiatives, motorists are asked to display a Vehicle Watch sticker on the front and rear windscreen of their vehicle, to indicate to the police that the vehicle should be stopped if seen on the road late at night—usually between midnight and 6am.

Responsibility for organising Vehicle Watch schemes rests with the police. Different forces, and divisions within forces, operate the schemes in different ways. Not surprisingly then, interviewee knowledge of Vehicle Watch was subject to regional variations. For example, 78 per cent of those from the Thames Valley area and 69 per cent of those from the North of England had not heard of Vehicle Watch, while 87 per cent from South Wales and 84 per cent from the Midlands had. Of the whole sample just over half (55%) had heard of Vehicle Watch.

After ensuring that interviewees understood the nature of Vehicle Watch they was asked if they thought the scheme would be effective in stopping cars being stolen. Most (82%) replied no; 15 per cent yes. A small number had taken cars carrying Vehicle Watch stickers and said they were not deterred by them. One 'didn't actually see the sticker' (No 115) until he had finished with the car. While another:

> Only used to nick cars with Vehicle Watch stickers in because as its got the sticker in they [the police] never bother.

Several suggested that the stickers could be peeled off (various methods were employed to achieve this) or covered up with another sticker, presumably put on the outside of the windscreen. And that in any event:

> When you go past you see coppers and they're just in the lay-by, not looking at you for Vehicle Watch stickers on.

In sum, the findings here offer little support for Vehicle Watch. They suggest that Vehicle Watch suffers from both theory failure—stickers do not appear to deter offenders—and implementation failure—as evidenced by offenders' lack of knowledge of the scheme. Two evaluations of Vehicle Watch are currently underway.

Summary

Of the present sample, over a third said car parks were their most favoured site for car theft—though many did not specify where they took cars from, or whether they chose different places during the day and at night. There is a recognisable bias in the vulnerability of certain makes and types of cars, but this is not as straightforward as some other studies have implied, being based on a combination of ease of theft, familiarity, owner behaviour, and offender preference. (The motive behind the theft will also affect which car is stolen—see Chapter 3.)

Vehicle security is seen as lamentably weak, offenders having little or no trouble in overcoming door and ignition locks. Alarm systems appear to be more effective in deterring offenders, but more information is needed on their relative effectiveness. The findings for Vehicle Watch from this study were not encouraging, though results from fuller evaluations will soon be available.

5 Criminal justice and deterrence

The criminal law has traditionally been seen as a primary counter-measure to car crime. This chapter covers offenders' views of the criminal justice system's response in terms of detection and punishment.

Offences and sanctions

If a vehicle is stolen to be sold, or parts of it are sold, the law of theft applies. Similarly, if a vehicle is broken into and property stolen from the car the offence is one of theft (and possibly criminal damage). However, if a vehicle is taken without intent to dispose of it (or parts of it), the necessary mental ingredient for theft—the 'intention of *permanently* depriving' the owner of it— is absent. Thus the temporary taker/joyrider cannot be convicted of the offence of *theft of the vehicle*; rather the offence is one of taking a conveyance without the owner's consent or other lawful authority (TWOC) under s 12 of the Theft Act 1968[1] (as amended by the Aggravated Vehicle-Taking Act, 1992).

The offence of taking without consent originally carried a maximum penalty of three years imprisonment, reduced to six months by virtue of s 37(1) of the Criminal Justice Act 1988. The 1988 Act, in line with a general shift towards summary trial to reduce waiting lists and the workload of the Crown Court, downgraded the offence to be triable only in the magistrates' courts. This attracted little attention at the time, but when car crime hit the headlines in 1991 the six month maximum sentence was attacked as inadequate, especially in cases where damage to property, death or injury had resulted.

Such was the level of concern, fuelled by daily media stories of high-speed police chases and road casualties involving illegally taken cars, that the introduction of tougher laws became inevitable. The Aggravated Vehicle-Taking Act came into force on 1 April 1992. The Act provides for an aggravated form of the TWOC offence under the 1968 Act—if, during the period when the vehicle was taken, it was driven dangerously, any damage to either the vehicle, or any other property was caused, or any injury was caused. The offence is triable either way and carries a maximum sentence of two years imprisonment

---

[1] For an account of earlier provisions see Appendix A.

or five years if death is caused. Both drivers and passengers may be convicted of the offence.

No fault element beyond the occurrence of the aggravated consequences needs to be proved in order to secure a conviction. A defendant can only escape liability if he can prove either that any aggravated consequences happened before he took the vehicle, or that he was not near it at the time.[1]

Justifying aims of punishment

Sanctions applied to car offenders may be intended to achieve one or more basic aims[2]—*retribution* (especially where death or personal injury has resulted); *individual deterrence* (dislike of the penalty designed to make the offender not want to repeat the offence); *incapacitation* (to stop further offending—eg, by disqualification from driving or a period in custody); and *rehabilitation or reform*.[3] There is also the question whether the example set by the law will have a general deterrent effect. Offenders in the study were asked for their views on aspects of the criminal justice response to car crime—particularly the law, detection and punishment. The data gathered here is of interest for the development of criminal justice responses to car crime.

Knowledge and perception of the law

Almost all of the interviewees (93%) displayed a general knowledge of the offences involved in what they did:

> TWOC, driving without insurance, driving while being disqualified—when you get chased it's . . . reckless driving.

Most referred to TWOC or TDA[4] and many added driving without a licence and insurance. Asked whether the taking of vehicles was wrong, only four per cent thought not. Of these one seemed unsure ('You know it's wrong but you don't seem to consider it wrong'), and two blamed car owners, either for not locking their vehicle or failing to get an alarm fitted.

Others reported not thinking about whether it was wrong to take cars (18%), but the majority (74%) acknowledged that it was:

---

[1] This has been criticised in some quarters as it throws the onus on defendants to prove that they are not guilty, rather than on the prosecution to prove guilt, prejudicing the presumption of innocence.
[2] Current sentencing policy, contained in The White Paper, 'Crime, Justice and Protecting the Public' (Home Office 1990), and reflected in the Criminal Justice Act 1991 provides that sentences should: express public abhorrence of the crime; punish the offender; protect the public; provide compensation for victims or reparation to the community; and deter against re-offending.
[3] The success or otherwise of the criminal justice system in achieving these aims is outside the scope of this study, but for a recent comprehensive analysis of the relative effectiveness of various measures in reducing re-offending in young people, see Bottoms (Ed) (forthcoming).
[4] The offence of taking and driving away a motor vehicle (TDA) preceded the TWOC offence. Many offenders and others still use the term.

> Because it's not your car. I respect cars now I've grown up a lot, I didn't respect them then. When you've got your own car—I mean a lot of the kids if they had their own car they wouldn't like it stolen.

A point graphically reinforced by one young man:

> You're taking somebody else's property. I actually know what it's like for somebody to steal my car and my motor bike—I went out and kicked their face in because I knew who it was.

Interestingly, eight of the sample (n=95) reported that the inconvenience caused for the car owner and the guilt that this generated was the worst part of their experience of car crime.

Despite an overwhelming view that taking cars was wrong, the majority of the sample (73%) did not consider car crime offences as serious:

> I see a lot of fuss going on with the joyriders robbing the cars and it's just property and I don't see no fuss about people themselves when they get bashed or murdered. At the end of the day you can kill someone and it's serious but you didn't go out to kill no one. Whether you've got a licence or not it's still an accident.

> You can always say there's a more serious offence. If you get a group in—like we've done this in probation—and put a list of offences on the board and say which is acceptable and which isn't things like stealing off your parents, you never do that, or rape. Murder is quite unacceptable.

For some, the fact that they caused little damage made the offences less serious:

> When I was nicking cars I was just parking them up . . . the damage I caused amounts to £150 tops. That's the door lock and ignition.

> Eighty per cent of the time the car comes back not damaged or a little bit of a snap here, it's not as if you're losing grands.

A few mentioned insurance:

> If you're insured, I wouldn't worry about it. If you're not insured it's tough shit—you should have been insured.

> Nine and a half out of 10 have got their cars insured, so if you steal their car or damage it or anything like that then they got their insurance. Sometimes I steal a car and set it on fire . . . so the people get their insurance, so it helps them out in a way.

One interviewee realised that having insurance might not be enough:

> I know you've got insurance but some people take a lot of pride in their cars and they put a lot of extras in it.

Of the 23 per cent who did feel that the offences were serious some based this view on the fact that offenders are often:

Too young and irresponsible to drive on the road. You are not cautious enough, you don't realise that you are dealing with a machine that can cause death and serious injury.

A small number of offenders expressed the view that attitudes to the offence had recently hardened:

When I was doing them, they weren't serious offences, but now they are. They've pinned down on them now. They're getting too hot.

At the time I did it, it wasn't seen as all that serious. It wasn't seen as a big sin.

Why should this be? Two reason were suggested: first, that widespread media attention relating to road casualties involving stolen cars had increased awareness of the dangers of joyriding; and secondly, that the increased penalties and the fact that offences may now be triable in the Crown Court marks them out as more serious.

Getting caught

Offenders' perceptions

Although 22 per cent of the sample had a feeling that they would be caught in the end, 74 per cent thought either that they would not be, or put it out of their mind:

When you actually do it, you don't think you are going to get caught. You think 'I'm not going to get caught'. You know if there was any risk of it you wouldn't do it.

Many felt that there was little chance of getting caught as 'the police have more important things to do'. And several said that if they drove sensibly and did not panic when they encountered the police there was little chance of them being apprehended:

As long as you drive normally you are usually ok—there's less chance of getting stopped. Some people when they see the police, they panic and put their foot down and they get noticed and the police check and find out its a stolen car.

Some claimed to have escaped apprehension so many times that they had ceased to worry about it:

Oh yes it goes through every joyrider's mind. For a while it used to put me off but I didn't get caught and it just went to the back of my mind.

At first yes. But if I can nick 300 cars in a month without being caught it doesn't say much for the police does it?

Such cavalier attitudes must be judged against the fact that only a fifth of the sample had in fact escaped contact with the police, 40 having been caught once or twice and 37 more than twice (Chapter 2). It may be that although many had

57

been involved with the police, in the context of the generally large number of offences claimed to have been committed, risks for particular incidents of theft seemed remote.

In any event, a high proportion (89%) said that the risk of apprehension did not deter them. Within this number 12 per cent thought that even if the police did get on to them that they would be able to get away; seven per cent claimed that the risk of being caught made things more exciting for them.

The risk of being caught

For a number of reasons, the actual chance of being caught and sanctioned can only be roughly estimated from official statistics on recorded crime and offenders proceeded against. For one, a proportion of offenders will come to the attention of the police, but will fall out of the tally of persons 'proceeded against' in that they will be informally cautioned, or be subject to a police decision to take no further formal action. Table 5.1 nonetheless gives a rough indication of risks of sanction based on 1990 figures. The shift should be noted between *offences* (Row A), and *offenders* (Row B onwards). Since there is no

Table 5.1
Number of offenders dealt with for theft and unauthorised taking of motor vehicles, 1990 (1)

A. Offences recorded by the police (2) (3)	494,000	
B. Offenders informally cautioned or no further action taken	unknown	
C. Offenders cautioned	10,000	
1. % offenders cautioned of offences cleared		7.8%
2. % offenders cautioned of recorded offences		2.0%
D. Offenders found guilty	22,000	
1. % offenders found guilty of offences cleared		16.8%
2. % offenders found guilty of recorded offences		4.4%
E. Offenders cautioned and found guilty (4)	32,000	
1. % offenders of offences cleared		24.6%
2. % offenders of recorded offences		6.4%

Notes:
1. Figures rounded to nearest 1,000. Percentages based on more precise numbers.
2. These offences cover both triable either way offences of theft of a motor vehicle, as well as the summary offence of 'unauthorised taking of a conveyance'. The vast majority of 'motor vehicles' will be cars. So too will 'conveyances', though the term also covers non-motorised vehicles (eg, trailers, farming conveyances, etc).
3. The number of offences recorded by the police is not an exact tally of offences committed since some offences will fail to enter police records because they are not reported by victims. In the case of theft of cars the number not reported is likely to be small.
4. There will also be a number of offenders who are taken to court but not found guilty, or whose cases are discharged; others will be informally cautioned by the police.

accurate count of the number of offences each offender is responsible for, the percentages given of those who are proceeded against are only suggestive of the 'likelihood of sanction'.

On the face of it, about six per cent (one in sixteen) of all offences committed result in an offender being either formally cautioned or convicted. This figure will give pause for thought in any debate about the certainty of sanction, though it probably underestimates the risk of sanction in a given year. Some offenders dealt with will have more than one offence set against them; and a number of others may be subject to some police action (eg, an informal caution), but not enter the formal count.

Police chases

Of particular concern in the policing of car theft are chases involving stolen vehicles and the danger they pose to offenders, the police and the public. Almost all the interviewees (91%) reported that they had been chased by the police, 72 per cent more than once. It is hard to say whether there was an element of exaggeration here.

Thirty-one per cent of the sample (n = 95) reported that getting caught or chased by the police was the worst thing about their experience of car crime (though being chased and getting away was the best experience for 14%). This challenges the view that offenders like to be chased, as does the fact that less than 10 per cent said they deliberately provoked the police into chasing them, just 'for the buzz':

> It was just like a game—me and the old bill, getting them to chase you and things like that.

> When the adrenalin starts flowing, that's it, there's no stopping. When you're being chased by the police and they've got their blue light flashing behind you, and you're going 80 miles an hour through a little street—I mean there's nothing that compares with it.

For many, being chased involved a mixture of fear and excitement:

> When you get chased by the police, it's very, very scary. Everyone says 'Oh I beat the police' and all that, but you actually get in a car with someone who's being chased and they're unbelievably scared. A lot of them are close to being physically sick. The stereo gets turned off, everyone sits and looks tense and nervous, no one says anything. Once you've got away from the police its 'Ah, yeah—great!' Its hard to think that five minutes ago they were almost being sick with fear.

> You notice they're behind you and you think 'shit'. The boys in the car start wondering what's going to happen, then I put my foot down and shoot off like that. The buzz that you get is unreal because you think you're on a good buzz, but you are also on a bad buzz because you're thinking 'Am I going to get caught?'.

For others, the thrill of the chase was the chance to test driving skills and cars were deliberately taken because they matched or exceeded the power of police cars:

> It's better in a fast car 'cos if you do get chased, if you're in something slow you've got no chance of getting away.

> You think 'I've got to get out of this', so you're giving it some and all the time you're eyes are everywhere. You're not looking straight ahead, you're all over the place; you need eyes in the back of your head . . . I mean some people just disregard it and just go and that's it, they don't consider anybody, but you've got to look for kids, cars coming the other way . . . you've got to be switched on the whole time, you haven't got time to think, you've got to be four steps ahead of everybody.

> If I ever get in a chase I head straight for the country because there's less cars to hit and get in the way. If you crash, you've got more places to go.

As mentioned already, offenders tended to overestimate their driving skills and to interpret police failure to catch them as evidence of inability rather than prudence:

> They say 'joyriders' or whatever you want to call them are bad drivers, but at the end of the day, the people behind the wheel of a stolen car can drive—he's got to be able to drive because the pressures on to get away from the police as soon as possible. It's not luck that they get away, they've got to be good drivers.

> I just took them (the police) through their paces on the council estates and lost them there.

A few people mentioned fear of the police beating them up as an extra incentive to get away:

> It's nerve wracking to put it mildly. You're hoping to God they're not going to catch you because most of the time now, you get a hell of a beating.

Some of the interviewees were critical of police tactics:

> They shouldn't be allowed to chase you, its just as simple as that . . . If it's a high performance car, the police don't usually touch it, they stay away because they know it's going to go quick.

> If a copper tries to pull you over, you just go like. They make it worse— they chase you and you panic and you do anything then, you just don't care, you want to get away from them, put your foot down.

> You've got to drive like hell to get away. They've got more powerful cars and the numbers have changed. Nowadays there are more police coming in to join a chase. They get on the radio and tell all their mates and they come

to rush in and help catch them. They're more alert about cars, so we've got to be twice as fast and quick thinking.

The police dilemma cannot be stressed too strongly. It may be that if the police adopt a policy of never chasing vehicles offenders may use it to their advantage and the public might be outraged; however, the safety of the public (and of the officers themselves) must be paramount.

Getting punished

Two questions were asked—did the interviewee think about what punishment could be expected if caught taking a car, and did that expectation act as a deterrent?

Perceived and actual risks of penalty

On the first question, 44 per cent of the sample reported thinking about what punishment they could expect if caught taking cars:

> I knew what the consequences were, well I had a reasonable idea what the consequences would be if I was caught.

A slightly larger number (47%) did not think about how they might be punished if caught, and nine per cent thought about it only sometimes:

> It (the thought of punishment) never entered my head. When I got caught, I got in trouble, I done my time and came out and I was at it again.

Not surprisingly, those in the 15–16 age range were least likely to think about punishment (58%). Less than a third of those aged over 26 years said the same. A disproportionately high number of the North of England sample (87%) said that they did not think about punishment.

A comparison can be made between what punishment the current offenders felt they would attract if caught,[1] and actual sentences meted out by the courts in 1990. The details are in Table 5.2. Offenders' perceptions are based on answers from slightly less than half of the sample (namely, those who said they kept possible punishment in mind). Actual sanctions are shown in two ways: (i) including the sizeable proportion who were taken to court but not convicted, and (ii) with these cases omitted. It is a moot point as to which comparison is best matched to offenders' perceptions of sanctions.

Compared to actual penalties, offenders *underestimate* their own chances of being cautioned or of getting a conditional discharge, whereas they *overestimate* considerably the likelihood of a custodial penalty. Such was the case with the present sample. This overestimation is of course pertinent to any policy option aiming to deter offenders from car theft by increasing the severity of

---

[1] The relevant questions were: 'Did you think you would be punished if you were caught taking a car? and 'What punishment did you think you would most likely receive?'.

Table 5.2
Sanctions against known offenders, 1990 (1) and perceptions of likely sentence

	Known offenders (i) %	Known offenders (ii) %	Offenders' perceptions %
Cautioned	24	31	15
Conditional discharge	9	11	4
Fine (2)	16	20	25
Probation	8	10	} 10
Community Service Order	7	9	
Custodial Sentence	9	11	46
Other sanctions	5	8	
Otherwise dealt with (3)	22		
Total	100	100	100

Notes:
(i)   Including those taken to court but not convicted.
(ii) Excluding those taken to court but not convicted.
1.   Based on numbers cautioned and dealt with in court for both the triable either way offence of theft of a motor vehicle, and the summary offence of 'unauthorised taking of a conveyance'.
2.   This covers those who responded 'fine and driving ban'. Most offenders mentioning a fine also mentioned a driving ban.
3.   An appreciable number of offenders whose case got to a magistrates' court had proceedings discontinued, were discharged, or had the charge withdrawn (31% all told). Similarly, of those whose case was heard in the Crown Court, some 9% were not given any of the sentences mentioned, mainly because they were acquitted.

sentences, for though the current sample were probably basing their judgements on their own experiences or those of friends, the evidence nonetheless suggests that offenders persist in stealing cars despite believing that the sanctions awaiting them if caught will be a good deal more serious than current judicial practice suggests will actually be the case.

Though numbers are limited when different age groups are considered, the indications are that younger offenders (aged 14–16) were the most prone to underestimate the likelihood of being cautioned if apprehended, and most likely to exaggerate the risk of a custodial sentence (Table 5.3). Those 17 or older appeared realistic in their judgements about the likelihood of being cautioned, although they were still more pessimistic about a custodial penalty than might be warranted—if not to as great a degree as young teenagers.

As mentioned, the most notable fact was the gross overestimation of custody, particularly among those in the youngest age group. This challenges the view that most offenders think that even if caught they will 'get away with it'.

Table 5.3
Sanctions against known offenders, 1990 (1) and perceptions of likely sentence, by age (2)

	Known offenders %	Known offenders %	Offenders' perceptions %
AGE 14–16			
Cautioned	54	61	33
Custodial Sentence	2	2	44
Other sanctions	32	37	
Otherwise dealt with (3)	12		
AGE 17–20			
Cautioned	9	12	14
Custodial Sentence	8	11	41
Other sanctions	59	77	
Otherwise dealt with (3)	24		
AGE 21+ (4)			
Cautioned	4	6	6
Custodial Sentence	17	26	53
Other sanctions	44	68	
Otherwise dealt with (3)	35		

Notes:
1. See footnote 1 to Table 5.2.
2. Based on responses from nine 14–16 year olds, twenty-two 17–20 year olds, and seventeen aged 21 or older.
3. See footnote 3 to Table 5.2.
4. Actual penalties based on all those aged 21 or older, compared to offenders in the current sample, the oldest of whom was 35.

Deterrent effect of sentences

As to whether expected penalties deterred, those which aimed to punish—fines, driving bans and custody—rated more highly than penalties with other aims. However, disqualification from driving and the imposition of penalty points are, as Spencer (forthcoming) points out:

> designed to be effective when the offender is old enough to obtain a legal driving licence—they do not mean much to the youths who had been given them.

Further, long periods of disqualification can have an adverse effect on a person's ability 'to go straight' when older, removing the opportunity to drive legitimately.

A number of people (15) said that the threat of custody had been enough to stop their offending, but of the 14 who had actually served one or more custodial sentences only one said that it had stopped him offending. The threat rather than the experience of custody therefore seems a stronger deterrent—assuming that those who reach custody do not differ markedly from those who give up before reaching that stage.

When those who thought about it were asked whether the expected punishment put them off taking cars, 21 per cent said yes and 73 per cent no. The reported deterrent effect varied with the type of punishment expected. None of those who expected to receive a caution, conditional discharge, probation or community service order reported being put off taking cars. One young man described probation as:

> Easy i'n' it? It's nothing, just go down the office once every two weeks, something like that. It doesn't help.

There was evidence from a few that cautions were seen as a let off:

> I had four cautions and an informal caution. I thought well I'm riding them at the moment, do you know what I mean? I'm above them because they keep giving me cautions.

> The first time's a caution . . . you just laugh at them really.

But for this offender nothing short of long custodial sentences seemed to be significant:

> I don't mind a couple of months but not 12 months, couple of years.

Of those who expected a fine coupled with a driving ban, 25 per cent reported being put off, for those expecting custody this rose to 50 per cent:

> I stopped because I got caught once and I knew for a fact I'd get sent down the next time.

The expectation of custody[1] was said by 15 of the sample to have been enough to deter them, although of the 14 offenders who had actually served one or more custodial sentences only one considered that it had stopped him offending:

> It wasn't very nice, it's a dirty place, you had to get down on your hands and knees and scrub the floors—you get about £2 a week and you can only buy half an ounce of tobacco to last you a week.

For others any deterrent effect seemed to be transient:

> I know it sounds mad but the last sentence that I got was 18 months, I done 12 months. When I came out it felt that I hadn't even been away. When I was doing the 12 months it was doing me head in I was thinking 'I'm not doing that again'. But as soon as I was on the streets again it was like I

---

[1] Detention in a Young Offender Institution for those aged 15–20 years and prison for 21 years and over.

hadn't been away, nothing had changed . . . The sentence didn't bother me after I got out.

Yet the futility of such a lifestyle was not lost on this particular young man (who was no longer taking cars):

> But now I think back and I think like I've lost years in gaol, doing three years, 18 months, I've lost years of me life.

Some considered that custody had no effect on their offending:

> I've been inside three times. You go in there the first time and there's lots of people like you in there, you get on with them, you can relate with them. You come out. OK so fair enough you're out, no big deal. You go in a second time, you come out. It's no penalty.

> I knew I'd be sent down. I got community service at one point, I breached it—I couldn't be bothered to go again. I went back to stealing cars and that and then I got six months. I came back out and did it again.

> I don't know what it was, but something said to me 'oh you've been put inside once like you've done the worst'.

> It was a joke last time, six months—it was a holiday for three months—lie back and put your feet up.

Several mentioned the notion that custodial institutions act as 'universities of crime':

> If you go in for one offence you learn four others and the trouble is you see the temptation to actually do it—'oh that lad told me you could do it this way. I wonder if I can?' And you'd be tempted to try it.

> When you are in prison like you find out a lot more things that you never knew. I went in there with my knowledge and I came out knowing three times as much.

Aggravated Vehicle-Taking Act 1992

The Aggravated Vehicle-Taking Bill was introduced amid wide publicity in late 1991 and came into force in April 1992, while the fieldwork for this study was in progress. Awareness of the new law was claimed by 69 per cent of the sample, while 70 per cent said that they were aware that penalties had been increased. Some misunderstood the new provisions, confusing them with aggravated burglary:

> I've heard of it but I can't understand how it can be done unless the owner of the car is sitting in the car with you; or pulling someone up, getting them to stop forcefully and pulling them out of the car.

> If you hit someone it would be aggravated something or other.

After ensuring that the interviewee was correctly informed of the aggravated offence and the penalties available the question was asked 'would it put you off at all?'. Over half considered that the new law would (32%) or might (23%) put them off offending. These figures, of course, relate only to how car offenders *said* they viewed the possible deterrent effect of the new law—which might have been invested with an element of 'fear of the unknown', due to its novelty and the wide publicity it was attracting at the time. Further research is needed, after the law has been in force for a reasonable period of time, to provide a more reliable assessment.

Six thought that the new law would make offenders who knew of the increased penalties more determined to escape apprehension and more likely to drive dangerously:

> All it means right if you were sitting behind the steering wheel and you've got a blue light behind you and you're looking at five years right nothing in front of you is going to stop you, if you hit kids you know what I mean. You want to get away. It might stop most of the joyriders, but I would just pinch a fast one.

> Naw, like cos when I pinch cars—100 mph through the streets but I'm always in control.

> People could drive a lot madder because they don't want to get caught.

> Yes, because you get four or five years just for nicking a car and having a laugh it's a bit steep. But you'll always get people wanting to beat the system, so for them it's going to be more of a challenge—they're going to make sure they don't get caught.

The view was expressed by one interviewee that the increased penalties could even enhance the status of the offence for some people:

> It's like grievous bodily harm is a serious offence and you can be seriously penalised for it. But people still do it, nevertheless, because a lot of people like to be able to say to somebody—'Yeah I got done for GBH'.

Most of the sample, however, thought that the new law would stop some offenders:

> Well I haven't pinched a car for a few months now but I've been in them. I would say out of 10 nearly four have stopped. The other six they just keep on doing it.

> A lot of the lads I've talked to in jail said they're not pinching cars when the new law comes in . . . whether it was jail talk 'cos they were locked up or what . . . I mean I suppose it'll knock joyriding on the head a lot. I mean they realise they're gonna get five years maximum.

Or at least make them more cautious:

There're a lot more cautious. They're going out of their way to be careful like, not doing anything dodgy until they are right out of the way, up on the moors or something.

Summary

Most offenders were in little doubt that stealing cars was morally wrong, though nearly three-quarters nonetheless felt that it was not a particularly serious form of offending. There was evidence that some offenders were responsive to the recent attention paid to car theft and now felt that the offence was considered more serious than it had once been. Most offenders claimed to be fairly immune to the risks of detection—though some 'macho' effect here cannot be discounted. Three-quarters put thoughts of being caught out of their mind, and nine out of ten were not deterred by the risk of apprehension anyway. Younger offenders were least likely to think about what punishment they might attract if caught. Contrasted with current sentencing practice, the chance of a custodial sentence was grossly overestimated, particularly by the youngest age group. For instance, 44 per cent of the 14–16 year old age group thought they would be sentenced to custody if caught, whereas of this age group sentenced in 1990, only two per cent were dealt with in this way.

Some measures were said to be of little deterrent value. None of those who expected a caution, conditional discharge, probation or community service order reported being deterred.

A quarter of those who expected a fine or driving ban saw this as a deterrent, though it is not possible to determine which was the greater threat. Half of those who expected custody felt similarly, though the *idea* of curtailment of liberty may be more potent than the actuality: only one of the fourteen offenders who had experienced custody was prepared to admit it had stopped him re-offending.

Over half the sample considered that the Aggravated Vehicle-Taking law would (32%) or might (23%) put them off taking cars. A minority (six) pointed to the danger of the new law making offenders drive more recklessly to avoid being caught, a problem already being experienced with police chases.

6 Discussion

The final chapter considers the implications of the research findings for four aspects of the response to car crime: first, the scope for curbing car crime through deterrent sentences; secondly, reducing the 'criminality' of those involved in car crime; thirdly, preventive measures aimed to reduce the opportunity for car crime—referred to here as situational prevention; and fourthly, the implementation of situational prevention methods.

Sentencing and the criminal justice system

It is often suggested that one possibility for reducing car crime might be for the courts to pass tougher sentences on offenders. However, both our research and earlier work on deterrent sentencing (Beyleveld, 1980; Brody, 1976) suggests that there is only limited scope here. This study helps throw some light on the reasons for this.

Increasing the risks of getting caught

The offenders in this sample were not asked to estimate the likelihood of their getting caught for any specific act of car theft (and their perceptions would have varied anyway depending on the particular circumstances of the theft). But, in estimating their 'career risk' generally, just over a fifth (22%) felt that they would be caught in the end, with the remainder either thinking they would escape detection altogether, or closing their mind to the issue.

Research suggests that one of the most important constraints on potential offenders is the belief that they will be caught (Walker, 1991; 1985). Most of the offenders in the study considered the prospect of being caught for stealing cars as highly unlikely—if they considered it at all. The admittedly rough estimate of a six per cent 'actual' chance of being sanctioned for an individual offence (ie, the proportion of recorded offences ending in a conviction or a caution) does little to belie offenders' optimism about escaping legal sanction.

How can the chances of apprehension be improved? Clarke (1991) describes various measures such as informant hotlines, sting operations, 'gotcha cars' and vehicle tracking devices. The present research can offer little in the way of comment on these initiatives, though Clarke concludes that while each may meet with some measure of success 'the scope for increasing the risks of detection and arrest is small'. As certain locations and types of car were identified as being at high risk of car theft it may be that policing can be better targeted and also, as offenders appeared confident that the police were unlikely to apprehend a sensibly driven stolen vehicle, officers given training in what to look for in identifying a vehicle as possibly stolen.

Penalties for car crime

Offenders were asked about the penalties they expected to receive if caught and how they saw these in terms of deterrence. For the half who did not think about how they would be punished if caught, penalties seemed of little consequence as a factor influencing offending. Of the remainder, 50 per cent said they were deterred by custody, and 25 per cent by fines/driving bans. None reported being deterred by probation, community service or cautions.

What offenders say and what they do may be very different things, of course. It is far from clear that greater use of custody would achieve any deterrent impact, as offenders already seem to overestimate the risks of a custodial sentence. On the other hand, offenders' apparent disregard of community penalties may reflect their ignorance about what is involved and the effect it may have on them.

Offenders' attitude to car theft

Most of the offenders interviewed considered it wrong to steal cars, but few felt the offences to be serious. Among their peers little or no stigma attached to their behaviour, indeed quite the opposite—status and respect rather than censure were apparent. A few offenders expressed the view that attitudes to car crime were hardening. This was based on increased media reporting of 'joyriding' deaths and the stiffer penalties introduced by the Aggravated Vehicle-Taking Act. This indicates that efforts to bring home to offenders the serious nature of the offences—through education and publicity—may be worth pursuing. It should include mundane details of the harm suffered by victims of car crime, as well as reports of shocking incidents involving stolen cars.

Such a policy may help to build a changing climate of offender opinion on the seriousness of car theft—a long-term educative effect of the type which has, for example, produced promising results in reducing drink-driving offences (see Riley, 1991). The significance of legislation such as the Aggravated Vehicle-Taking Act, aside from retribution or 'just deserts', may lie not so much in any deterrent pay-off, but in the longer term shifts in attitudes that it helps to achieve.

When interviewees were asked why they had given up car crime, or why other people might give up, increased maturity and responsibility were given much greater prominence in their answers than the effect of penal sanctions. Linking this with the group nature of much car theft, the influence of peers in starting off the car crime career, and the young age of first involvement, underlines the need for early diversionary strategies. These are considered in the next section of this chapter.

Reducing criminality

The second group of preventive options aims to reduce the motivation to offend, rather than to obstruct or deter motivated offenders.

The social background of offenders

Chapter 2 painted a grim but familiar backdrop against which much young offending occurs: high truancy rates, low educational attainment, high unemployment, lack of leisure facilities and so on (*cf* Briggs, 1991; Spencer, forthcoming). A third of our sample came from families in which offending was common, and whilst only a small proportion of parents were unconcerned about their children's involvement in crime, many were reported as powerless to intervene. Thus, on the one hand, there were few legitimate opportunities for excitement and financial gain to match the pay-offs from car crime; and, on the other, the social pressures to prevent criminal involvement were weak.

The strong contrast between the offenders' views of the skill and daring involved in their car crime activities and the aimlessness and lack of commitment with which they claim to approach the rest of their lives needs to be understood more fully and is perhaps central to any offender based policy initiatives.

Some would see widespread crime to be an inevitable fact of life in the socially-deprived areas from which most of our offenders came; and they would argue that the only solution lies in improvements in educational provision, employment prospects, and housing. Leaving aside the question whether expenditure in 'urban renewal' always achieves the desired effect, there are obvious difficulties in raising sufficient money to have any impact on a national scale. Whatever the case, considerations of crime reduction are likely to play only a secondary role in the development of social and economic policies to tackle deprivation.

Offender-based strategies

Another approach to reducing criminality is to target efforts on those who have already been identified as offenders. The orthodoxy of the 1970s and early 80s was that very little could be done by way of effective rehabilitation, (Martinson 1974, Brody 1976). However, it now seems clear that the research evidence does not support the generalisation that 'nothing works', and several studies have been able to demonstrate some success for various forms of probation supervision. It is beyond the scope of this report to review this body of research as it relates to 'generalist' offenders—which will include many people who have been convicted of vehicle crimes. Summaries of relevant work are to be found in

Raynor (1988) and Roberts (1989). Schemes targeted at car crime offenders specifically are considered below.

Car crime offenders

Our research has underlined three distinctive features of car theft. First, it offers adolescents an unusual and potent mix in terms of excitement, status and self-esteem. Many other acquisitive crimes have an element of psychological pay-off (eg burglary: Nee and Taylor, 1988; Bennett and Wright, 1984; and robbery: Feeney, 1986), but they do not compare with the thrills attainable in driving a stolen 'performance' car at speed. (Some of those interviewed reported that the fear and speed of a chase further increased excitement.) Secondly, there is a considerable degree of specialisation amongst those involved in car theft, in that their involvement in crime is largely restricted to offences involving vehicles. If their accounts are genuine—and they are at least consistent—the criminal activity of specialists is rooted in a strong interest in cars; they have early and sustained aspirations to jobs involving cars; and they begin driving illegally on the road at an early age.

The challenge for effective offender-based intervention is to find some form of legal alternative to car theft which manages to provide groups of young car-obsessed offenders (or those at risk of offending) with comparable excitement and interest. 'Motor projects' may be an option with the right ingredients. These are increasingly being set up by probation services as well as by some voluntary groups. Although they take several forms, they generally involve the teaching of driving and car maintenance skills, interspersed with messages about the risks of car theft, the impact on victims and the consequences for offenders. Some of the more elaborate schemes are linked with 'banger racing'. A well-run motor project might be seen as an example of 'reintegrative shaming' (Braithwaite, 1989). Braithwaite suggests that in order for law effectively to reduce crime, an element of shaming is necessary. And in order to reduce deviant behaviour, the shaming must be 'reintegrative' rather than 'disintegrative'. In other words, its procedures must aim to redirect the individual back into the non-offending community rather than reinforce his links and identity with the criminal subculture. No formal evaluations of motor projects are as yet available, though some Home Office-funded research is under way.

A third feature of car theft revealed by the research is the ease of progression from casual and hedonistic involvement to more organised profit making at a very early age. Offenders consistently referred to an 'apprenticeship' stage of the car crime career, both in this and other research (McCullough *et al.*, 1990). This suggests that there may be an important and short period of time— apparently some six months to a year after initial involvement in car theft— within which to divert young offenders before they become skilled and well-entrenched in the habit.

71

Situational prevention

The final set of options considered here are those which can be grouped under the heading of 'situational prevention'. These involve making the offenders' task more difficult by reducing the opportunities for offending.

The risk a vehicle runs of theft depends on four main factors. The first is the locations in which the car is parked—which is returned to. The second is actual or perceived ease of theft. To an extent it is older cars which are considered the easiest targets, though some current newer models get considerable mention too, target-hardening measures being particularly relevant to these—also returned to. The third factor is the extent to which offenders are familiar with the make of car. To a degree, the risk of theft is determined not by the objective difficulty of stealing it but by whether offenders have had opportunities to practice the techniques that work best for that car. The implication here is that models with high-volume sales should be particularly well-protected by manufacturers. The fourth factor is the appeal of the car's image to offenders—which depends to a large extent on the design brief, as well as the way in which it is advertised and marketed by the manufacturer. Assuming that manufacturers continue to produce and market sporty cars which offer exciting, aggressive images there is no doubt that offenders will continue to aspire to steal them. These and other high risk cars will need to be better protected. Car crime was clearly considered by most of the offenders in the sample as glamorous and exciting. How far advertising and marketing has created or reinforced this view is debatable, but the recent trend away from performance/thrills in advertising is a development to be encouraged, particularly considering the possible additional benefits for road safety generally.

Findings from this and other research, especially the *Car Theft Index*, allows high-risk types and makes of vehicle to be identified. For new models, policy is straightforward—manufacturers must be encouraged to improve security. For older high-risk cars, the potential is less obvious. Owners could be made more aware of their car's vulnerability, though many may be unwilling or unable to afford to invest in additional security equipment.

Locks

The major development in lock security has been the introduction of 'deadlocks' for car doors—which cannot be unlocked from inside the car, only from outside with a key. Few of the offenders in the sample had come across these locks; those who had agreed that they would be more difficult, although by no means impossible to overcome—eg, by ripping the entire lock from the door or breaking a window to get in. This of course would give a visible sign that the car had been stolen and many offenders might feel uncomfortable about not being able to open the door to make a quick escape. On balance, deadlocks would receive endorsement from this study, and indeed the Home Office has for some time been pressing manufacturers to introduce them as standard on new cars.

Alarms

The study showed that alarms can deter. It also indicated that more information is needed on the relative efficiency of types and makes, and the ability or otherwise of offenders to deactivate alarms. Further, the problem of false alarms needs to be addressed—as much to ensure that notice is taken of alarms as to reduce the social cost of noise pollution.

Immobilisers

The study did not specifically address the effectiveness of immobilisers, which incapacitate the vehicle by cutting off either the fuel or electrical supply to the engine—preventing the car being driven away. Offenders who mentioned immobilisers did so as a component of 'better type' alarm systems presenting a further impediment to stealing the car. Fully integrated into a car's electronic management system, immobilisers would promise to be very effective. Any customer resistance to immobilisers (eg because they might be thought to present a danger in 'normal' driving situations) could probably be overcome with better design and a careful 'sales pitch'.

Theft from cars

'Pull out' radio/cassette players seemed to offer some protection, though from offenders' accounts owner inertia still leaves many opportunities for theft, particularly from owners who slide the radio out but leave it in the car. Recent attempts to overcome this with modified systems which require only the smaller and more portable control panel to be removed promise to be helpful. It will remain to be seen whether these panels are prone to being lost or broken, and whether they could be replaced by thieves if cheap enough.

Newer radio/cassette players with electronic security coding are another way forward, though the interviewees offered little comment on them. (A code has to be punched in before the radio/cassette can be played and if power to the unit is disrupted, the code no longer works, and has to be reset.) Coded equipment has been shown to be effective in reducing thefts in Australia (NRMA, 1990), though to start with offenders did not know the equipment would be useless without the code. Also, the codes in early models could be erased by leaving the radio/cassette overnight in a freezer. Coded systems need to be clearly marked and backed up with window stickers. It may also be worth encouraging manufacturers to fit audio systems which can be dispersed throughout the car to make them more difficult to steal (Clarke, 1991).

Wheel protection

Results here have shown stylish wheels to be a popular target of theft, and easily removed. Their popularity stems from the existence of a ready market of owners with basic or older model cars keen to upgrade their vehicle. Protection can be afforded by locking wheel nuts, which should be fitted by manufacturers, and by indelible marking with a vehicle identification number, to allow the police to trace stolen wheels more easily. Evidence suggests that factory marking of components is successful in reducing thefts of car parts, but manufacturers are said to be hostile to the idea, mainly on grounds of cost (Clarke, 1991).

Linked to this is the need to curtail the numerous outlets for the proceeds of car crime, from both casual (radio/cassette players etc) and more 'professional' pursuits (either whole cars or their parts). Unfortunately, the demand for such merchandise is so great that this is likely to be very difficult. Foster (1990) describes the activities of one such outlet in South-East London in detail, where stolen car radios can be sold all day, and on average two stolen cars per week and the parts of several are dealt with. This said, sustained effort to increase control over second-hand car and car parts trading and scrap-yard dealing must have some pay-off.

Vehicle Watch

The study suggests that Vehicle Watch has failed as yet to have any significant impact on car crime offenders in this study, though future success would not be ruled out by these results. At present, implementation is patchy and inconsistent; for instance, in some areas stickers are free, in others they have to be paid for. Some degree of national coordination might result in wider take-up and better sharing of good practice. Vehicle Watch also needs to be evaluated properly.

Car parks and street parking

This and other studies have suggested that cars parked in car parks and those parked overnight in the street are frequently targeted by thieves, though without an accurate 'baseline' of number of cars parked in different locations at different times, this can only be a rough guide. The risks of on-street residential parking could be reduced by longer-term measures to improve street lighting and to incorporate secure parking provision in housing design. The more immediate option—which has been incorporated into the publicity initiatives mounted in Car Crime Prevention Year—is to encourage those with access to garages or off-street parking to make regular use of it and to promote busy rather than quiet parking sites where possible.

The subject of car park vulnerability has been extensively covered in a recent Home Office study (Webb et al., 1992). Our offenders' accounts endorse the recommendations made there for better security and car park management. There may well be added benefits in terms of reducing other crime, and for lessening the sense of insecurity which certain types of public car parks induce, particularly among women.

Implementing preventive measures

Crime prevention messages have been directed primarily at manufacturers and owners—manufacturers being encouraged to make more effort, owners to take more care.

Car manufacturers

According to the offenders interviewed, car security is lamentably weak. The study confirms the ease with which offenders are able to enter and start vehicles. The results here suggest that most cars can be stolen using a few simple tools, with door and ignition/steering locks offering little resistance. Action by manufacturers seems long overdue. Several areas of improvement have already been mentioned (eg locks, alarms, immobilisers, and wheel protection); and others have been singled out elsewhere (eg boot security, and laminated side windows, Southall and Ekblom, 1985).

Motor manufacturers have traditionally been reluctant to improve car security—arguing that customers are resistant to the cost and that crime prevention is the job of the police. However, the 1988 British Crime Survey found that 64 per cent of car buyers would be willing to pay for extra security (Clarke, 1991) and manufacturers are now coming under increasing pressure—both from central government and insurance companies—to accept responsibility for enhanced car security. This, together with anticipation of EC regulations and customer concern about car crime, all appear to be making manufacturers reconsider their position. There are signs that better security is now being incorporated into car design. Material on risks and good security practice has featured in many of the publicity initiatives mounted during Car Crime Prevention Year, though continuing efforts will no doubt be needed to influence drivers' behaviour.

How far improved security will lead to spiralling levels of sophistication between thieves and manufacturers remains to be seen. Professional thieves are likely to pose the biggest 'displacement' threat, but the evidence of this study suggests that other offenders might be outwitted. Only simple tools were used by the interviewees and none reported using 'slim jims' or universal key sets, let alone electronic gadgetry such as 'code grabbers' that open central locking systems and override alarms. This leaves aside, however, the question of displacement to other less well-protected vehicles. If better security of newer cars ensues, this will need to be monitored, for instance through examining changes in the age of vehicles stolen.

Car owners

Although purchasers of new vehicles may well benefit from better levels of protection against car theft, it will be some years before offenders are faced with only 'harder' targets. For instance, by 1996, roughly 40 per cent of cars on the road will have been manufactured in 1992 or later, which will still leave nearly 15 million older targets available.[1] Older vehicles may be increasingly targeted due to displacement from better-secured, newer vehicles, as happened with the introduction of steering column locks in the early 1970s (Mayhew *et al*, 1976).

What advice can be offered to those who own the older vehicles? Publicity campaigns have been mounted to increase public awareness of car crime. Owners have been encouraged, among other things, to secure their cars and remove valuables, or at least lock them out of sight in the boot. This may reduce risks but not eliminate them. Findings from this study show that locked cars are easily broken into and many offenders mentioned looking in car boots for property to steal ('booting' as they termed it)—an easy task in hatchbacks and in modern saloons with access available through the rear seat back.

Owners need to be given fuller information on car crime to enable them to assess their vulnerability to car theft. Such information could usefully be based on theft risks for particular vehicles and parking locations, augmented by better promotion of available types of security equipment. This should allow owners some control over the risks they run. For example, a person who leaves an older, high-risk vehicle in a quiet street at night, and in a public car park all day would be well advised to fit an alarm or even change models.

Better information is needed on alarms, and this should be publicly available. Owners may be reluctant to purchase or be confused by the bewildering variety and complexity of the systems on offer. Offender responses here indicate that some alarms are more effective than others. Informed owner choice is essential.

In sum, then, the limits of situational prevention must be recognised. Not everybody is willing or able to take the most effective preventive steps. Some offenders will be thwarted by physical measures, some will overcome them, and others will simply target more vulnerable vehicles. Nevertheless, important advances are being made for new vehicles which offer the prospect of lower risks for their owners at least.

---

[1] Estimated from Department of Transport, 1991: 118.

Appendix A   The law

In the early days of the motor car the charge brought in cases of wrongful taking of vehicles was theft of the petrol which had been used. But, as offences multiplied with the increasing volume of motor vehicles on the roads, concern grew over the inadequacy of the law to properly cover such conduct. By the end of the 1920s there were more than two million vehicles registered in Britain and much disquiet expressed about unauthorised joyriding. New legislative provisions contained in s 28 of the Road Traffic Act 1930 introduced the offence of taking and driving away 'any motor vehicle without having the consent of the owner thereof or other lawful authority' (TDA). The maximum penalty was 12 months imprisonment.

By the 1960s the number of motor vehicles licensed had passed 10 million, car ownership had widened its base considerably and the motor car had become the symbol of prosperity. Unauthorised taking of vehicles had also escalated. Yet the law contained in the 1930 Act remained basically unchanged. The TDA provisions had been re-enacted by s 217 of the Road Traffic Act 1960 and were later amended by the Road Traffic Act 1962 to include a 'passenger' 'who knowing that a motor vehicle has been so taken . . . drives it or allows himself to be carried in or on it', but this was not sufficient to silence the critics.

The 1960s which saw rapidly expanding vehicle numbers and the highest ever level of road casualties in peacetime (7,985 deaths in 1966) precipitated several initiatives aimed at better regulation of motor vehicle use and misuse. New provisions were introduced by s 12 of the Theft Act 1968, which made it an offence to take a conveyance without the owner's consent or lawful authority. The maximum penalty was three years imprisonment.

References

Bennett, T. and Wright, R. (1984). *Burglars on Burglary*. Aldershot: Gower.

Beyleveld, D. (1980). *A Bibliography on General Deterrence Research*. Farnborough: Saxon House.

Bottoms, A. E. (Ed.). (Forthcoming). *Community Penalties for Young Offenders*.

Braithwaite, J. (1989). *Crime, Shame and Re-integration*. Cambridge: Cambridge University Press.

Briggs, J. (1991). *A Profile of the Juvenile Joyrider*. Durham: University of Durham.

Brody, S. R. (1976). *The Effectiveness of Sentencing: a review of the literature*. Home Office Research Study No. 35. London: HMSO.

Carroll, J. and Weaver, F. (1986), 'Shoplifters' perceptions of crime opportunities: a process tracing study'. In, Cornish, D. and Clarke, R. (Eds.), *The Reasoning Criminal*. New York: Springer-Verlag.

Clarke, R. (1991). *Preventing Vehicle Theft: a policy oriented review of the literature*. Edinburgh: Scottish Home and Health Department.

Cornish, D. and Clarke, R. (1986). *The Reasoning Criminal*. New York: Springer-Verlag.

Department of Transport (1991). *Transport statistics Great Britain 1991*. London: HMSO.

Farrington, D. P., Snyder, H. N. and Finnegan, T. A. (1988). 'Specialisation in juvenile court careers'. *Criminology*, 26: 461–487.

Feeney, F. (1986). 'Robbers as decision-makers'. In, Cornish, D. and Clarke, R. (Eds.), *The Reasoning Criminal*. New York: Springer-Verlag.

Foster, J. (1990). *Villains, Crime and Community in the Inner City*. London: Routledge.

Gibbens, T. C. N. (1957). 'Car thieves'. *British journal of Delinquency*, VIII: 257–265.

Goddard, E. (1991). *Drinking in England and Wales in the late 1980's*. London: HMSO.

Gow, J. and Peggrem, A. (1991). Unpublished questionnaire survey. Barnado's '175' Project, Newport.

Gulliver, N. (1991). Unpublished questionnaire survey. Northumbria Probation Service.

Home Office. (1988). *Standing Conference on Crime Prevention: Report of the Working Group on Car Crime*. London: Home Office.

Home Office (1990). *Crime, Justice and Protecting the Public*. London: HMSO.

Home Office Statistical Department. (1985). *Criminal Careers of those Born in 1953, 1958, 1965*. Statistical Bulletin 7/85. London: HMSO.

Houghton, G. (1992). *Car Theft in England and Wales: the Home Office Car Theft Index*, CPU Paper 33. London: Home Office.

Klein, M. (1984). 'Offense specialisation and versatility among juveniles'. *British journal of Criminology*, 24: 185–194.

Martinson, R. (1974). 'What works? Questions and answers about prison reform'. *Public Interest*, 35: 22–54.

Mayhew, P., Elliott, D. and Dowds, L. (1989). *The 1988 British Crime Survey*, Home Office Research Study N. 111. London: HMSO.

McCullough, D. and Schmidt, T. (1990). '"Joyriding" in West Belfast' in **McCullough** *et al* (1990).

McCullough, D., Schmidt, T. and Lockhart, B. (1990). *Car Theft in Northern Ireland: recent studies on a persistent problem.* Cirac Paper No. 2. Belfast: Extern Organisation.

National Opinion Poll. (1991). *Political, Social and Economic Review, No. 89.* (December) London: NOP.

Nee, C. and Taylor, M. (1988a). 'Residential Burglary in the Republic of Ireland: Some support for the situational approach'. In, Tomlinson, M., Varley, A. and McCullagh, C. (Eds.), *Whose Law and Order?* (1988) Sociological Association of Ireland.

Nee, C. and Taylor, M. (1988b). 'Residential burglary in the Republic of Ireland: a situational perspective'. *Howard Journal of Criminal Justice,* 27: 105–116.

NOP. (1990). *Young Peoples' Attitudes to Crime.* Unpublished report carried out for BBC television's 'Reportage' programme.

Phillpotts, G. J. O. and Lancucki, L. B. (1979). *Previous convictions, sentence and reconviction.* Home Office Research Study No. 53. London: HMSO.

Raynor, P. (1988). *Probation as an alternative to custody: a case study.* Aldershot: Avebury.

Riley, D. (1991). *Drink Driving: the effects of enforcement,* Home Office Research Study No. 121, London: HMSO.

Roberts, C. H., (1989). *Young Offender Project: first evaluation report.* Hereford and Worcester Probation Service.

Smyth, G. (1990). *Greater Manchester Probation/Police Car Crime Campaign: Results of Probation Offenders Questionnaire,* Greater Manchester Probation Service (unpublished).

Southall, D. and Ekblom, P. (1985). *Designing for Car Security: towards a crime free car.* Crime Prevention Unit Paper No. 4. London: Home Office.

Spencer, E. (Forthcoming). *Car Crime and Young People on a Sunderland Housing Estate,* Crime Prevention Unit Paper. London: Home Office.

Stander, J., Farrington, D. P., Hill, G. and Altham, P. M. E. (1989). 'Markov chain analysis of specialisation in criminal careers'. *British Journal of Criminology*, 29: 317–335.

Tarling, R. (1991). *Offending: data, models and interpretations.* Unpublished PhD thesis.

Walker, N. (1985). *Sentencing: theory, law and practice.* London: Butterworth.

Walker, N. (1991). *Why Punish?* Oxford: Oxford University Press.

Webb, B., Brown, B. and Bennett, T. (1992). *Preventing Car Crime in Car Parks.* CPU Paper No. 34. London: Home Office.

Webb, B. and Laycock, G. (1992). *Tackling Car Crime: the nature and extent of the problem.* Crime Prevention Unit Paper No. 32. London: Home Office.

West, D. J. and Farrington, D. P. (1977). *The Delinquent Way of Life.* London: Heinemann.

Publications

Titles already published for the Home Office

Studies in the Causes of Delinquency and the Treatment of Offenders (SCDTO)

1. *Prediction methods in relation to borstal training. Hermann Mannheim and Leslie T. Wilkins. 1955. viii + 276pp. (11 340051 9).
2. *Time spent awaiting trial. Evelyn Gibson. 1960. v + 45pp. (34-368-2).
3. *Delinquent generations. Leslie T. Wilkins. 1960. iv + 20pp. (11 340053 5).
4. *Murder. Evelyn Gibson and S. Klein. 1961. iv + 44pp. (11 340054 3).
5. *Persistent criminals. A study of all offenders liable to preventive detention in 1956. W. H. Hammond and Edna Chayen. 1963. ix + 237pp. (34-368-5).
6. *Some statistical and other numerical techniques for classifying individuals. P. McNaughton-Smith. 1965. v + 33pp (34-368-6).
7. *Probation research: a preliminary report. Part I. General outline of research. Part II. Study of Middlesex probation area (SOMPA). Steven Folkard, Kate Lyon, Margaret M. Carver and Erica O'Leary. 1966. vi + 58pp. (11 340374 7).
8. *Probation research: national study of probation. Trends and regional comparisons in probation (England and Wales). Hugh Barr and Erica O'Leary. 1966. vii + 51pp. (34-368-8).
9. *Probation research. A survey of group work in the probation service. Hugh Barr. 1966. vii + 94pp. (34-368-9).
10. *Types of delinquency and home background. A validation study of Hewitt and Jenkins' hypothesis. Elizabeth Field. 1967. vi + 21pp. (34-368-10).
11. *Studies of female offenders. No. 1—Girls of 16–20 years sentenced to borstal or detention centre training in 1963. No. 2—Women offenders in the Metropolitan Police District in March and April 1957. No. 3—A description of women in prison on January 1, 1965. Nancy Goodman and Jean Price. 1967. v + 78pp. (34-368-11).
12. *The use of the Jesness Inventory on a sample of British probationers. Martin Davies. 1967. iv + 20pp. (34-368-12).
13. *The Jesness Inventory: application to approved school boys. Joy Mott. 1969. iv + 27pp. (11 340063 2).

Home Office Research Studies (HORS)

1. *Workloads in children's departments. Eleanor Grey. 1969. vi + 75pp. (11 340101 9).
2. *Probationers in their social environment. A study of male probationers aged 17–20, together with an analysis of those reconvicted within twelve months. Martin Davies. 1969. vii + 204pp. (11 340102 7).
3. *Murder 1957 to 1968. A Home Office Statistical Division report on murder in England and Wales. Evelyn Gibson and S. Klein (with annex by the Scottish Home and Health Department on murder in Scotland). 1969. vi + 94pp. (11 340103 5).
4. *Firearms in crime. A Home Office Statistical Division report on indictable offences involving firearms in England and Wales. A. D. Weatherhead and B. M. Robinson. 1970. vii + 39pp. (11 340104 3).

81

5. *Financial penalties and probation. Martin Davies. 1970. vii + 39pp. (11 340105 1).

6. *Hostels for probationers. A study of the aims, working and variations in effectiveness of male probation hostels with special reference to the influence of the environment on delinquency. Ian Sinclair. 1971. ix + 200pp. (11 340106 X).

7. *Prediction methods in criminology—including a prediction study of young men on probation. Frances H. Simon. 1971. xi + 234pp. (11 340107 8).

8. *Study of the juvenile liaison scheme in West Ham 1961–65. Marilyn Taylor. 1971. vi + 46pp. (11 340108 6).

9. *Exploration in after-care. I—After-care units in London, Liverpool and Manchester. Martin Silberman (Royal London Prisoners' Aid Society) and Brenda Chapman. II—After-care hostels receiving a Home office grant. Ian Sinclair and David Snow (HORU). III—St. Martin of Tours House, Aryeh Leissner (National Bureau for Co-operation in Child Care). 1971. xi + 140pp. (11 340109 4).

10. *A survey of adoption in Great Britain. Eleanor Grey in collaboration with Ronald M. Blunden. 1971. ix + 168pp. (11 340110 8).

11. *Thirteen-year-old approved school boys in 1962s. Elizabeth Field, W. H. Hammond and J. Tizard. 1971. ix + 46pp. (11 340111 6).

12. *Absconding from approved schools. R. V. G. Clarke and D. N. Martin. 1971. vi + 146pp. (11 340112 4).

13. *An experiment in personality assessment of young men remanded in custody. H. Sylvia Anthony. 1972. viii + 79pp. (11 340113 2).

14. *Girl offenders aged 17–20 years. I—Statistics relating to girl offenders aged 17–20 years from 1960 to 1970. II—Re-offending by girls released from borstal or detention centre training. III—The problems of girls released from borstal training during their period on after-care. Jean Davies and Nancy Goodman. 1972,. v + 77pp. (11 340114 0).

15. *The controlled trial in institutional research—paradigm or pitfall for penal evaluators? R. V. G. Clarke and D. B. Cornish. 1972. v + 33pp. (11 340115 9).

16. *A survey of fine enforcement. Paul Softley. 1973. v + 65pp. (11 340116 7).

17. *An index of social environment—designed for use in social work menum research. Martin Davies. 1973. vi + 63pp. (11 340117 5).

18. *Social enquiry reports and the probation service. Martin Davies and Andrea Knopf. 1973. v + 49pp. (11 340118 3).

19. *Depression, psychopathic personality and attempted suicide in a borstal sample. H. Sylvia Anthony. 1973. viii + 44pp. (0 11 340119 1).

20. *The use of bail and custody by London magistrates' courts before and after the Criminal Justice Act 1967. Frances Simon and Mollie Weatheritt. 1974. vi + 78pp. (0 11 340120 5).

21. *Social work in the environment. A study of one aspect of probation practice. Martin Davies, with Margaret Rayfield, Alaster Calder and Tony Fowles. 1974. ix + 151pp. (0 11 340121 3).

22. *Social work in prison. An experiment in the use of extended contact with offenders. Margaret Shaw. 1974. viii + 154pp. (0 11 340122 1).

23. *Delinquency amongst opiate users. Joy Mott and Marilyn Taylor. 1974. vi + 31pp. (0 11 340663 0).

24. *IMPACT. Intensive matched probation and after-care treatment. Vol. I—The design of the probation experiment and an interim evaluation. M. S. Folkard, A. J. Fowles, B. C. McWilliams, W. McWilliams, D. D. Smith, D. E. Smith and G. R. Walmsley. 1974. v + 54pp. (0 11 340664 9).

25. *The approved school experience. An account of boys' experiences of training under differing regimes of approved schools, with an attempt to evaluate the effectiveness of that training. Anne B. Dunlop. 1974. vii + 124pp. (0 11 340665 7).

26. *Absconding from open prisons. Charlotte Banks, Patricia Mayhew and R. J. Sapsford. 1975. viii + 89pp. (0 11 340666 5).

27. *Driving while disqualified. Sue Kriefman. 1975. vi + 136pp. (0 11 340667 3).

28. *Some male offenders' problems. I—Homeless offenders in Liverpool. W. McWilliams. II—Casework with short-term prisoners. Julie Holborn. 1975. x + 147pp. (0 11 340668 1).

29. *Community service orders. K. Pease, P. Durkin, I. Earnshaw, D. Payne and J. Thorpe. 1975. viii + 80pp. (0 11 340669 X).

30. *Field Wing Bail Hostel: the first nine months. Frances Simon and Sheena Wilson. 1975. viii + 55pp. (0 11 340670 3).

31. *Homicide in England and Wales 1967–1971. Evelyn Gibson. 1975. iv + 59pp. (0 11 340753 X).

32. *Residential treatment and its effects on delinquency. D. B. Cornish and R. V. G. Clarke. 1975. vi + 74pp. (0 11 340672 X).

33. *Further studies of female offenders. Part A: Borstal girls eight years after release. Nancy Goodman, Elizabeth Maloney and Jean Davies. Part B: The sentencing of women at the London Higher Courts. Nancy Goodman, Paul Durkin and Janet Halton. Part C: Girls appearing before a juvenile court. Jean Davies. 1976. vi + 114pp. (0 11 340673 8).

34. *Crime as opportunity. P. Mayhew, R. V. G. Clarke, A. Sturman and J. M. Hough. 1976. vii + 36pp. (0 11 340674 6).

35. *The effectiveness of sentencing: a review of the literature. S. R. Brody. 1976. v + 89pp. (0 11 340675 4).

36. *IMPACT. Intensive matched probation and after-care treatment. Vol. II—The results of the experiment. M. S. Folkard, D. E. Smith and D. D. 1976. xi + 40pp. (0 11 340676 2).

37. *Police cautioning in England and Wales. J. A. Ditchfield. 1976. v + 31pp. (0 11 340677 0).

38. *Parole in England and Wales. C. P. Nuttall, with E. E. Barnard, A. J. Fowles, A. Frost, W. H. Hammond, P. Mayhew, K. Pease, R. Tarling and M. J. Weatheritt. 1977. vi + 90pp. (0 11 340678 9).

39. *Community service assessed in 1976. K. Pease, S. Billingham and I. Earnshaw. 1977. vi + 29pp. (0 11 340679 7).

40. *Screen violence and film censorship: a review of research. Stephen Brody. 1977. vii + 179pp. (0 11 340680 0).

41. *Absconding from borstals. Gloria K. Laycock. 1977. v + 82pp. (0 11 340681 9).

42. *Gambling: a review of the literature and its implications for policy and research. D. B. Cornish. 1978. xii + 284pp. (0 11 340682 7).

43. *Compensation orders in magistrates' courts. Paul Softley. 1978. v + 41pp. (0 11 340683 5).

44. *Research in criminal justice. John Croft. 1978. iv + 16pp. (0 11 340684 3).

45. *Prison welfare: an account of an experiment at Liverpool. A. J. Fowles. 1978. v + 34pp. (0 11 340685 1).

46. *Fines in magistrates' courts. Paul Softley. 1978. v + 42pp. (0 11 340686 X).

47. *Tackling vandalism. R. V. Clarke (editor), F. J. Gladstone, A. Sturman and Sheena Wilson (contributors). 1978. vi + 91pp. (0 11 340687 8).

48. *Social inquiry reports: a survey. Jennifer Thorpe. 1979. vi + 55pp. (0 11 340688 6).

49. *Crime in public view. P. Mayhew, R. V. G. Clarke, J. N. Burrows, J. M. Hough and S. W. C. Winchester. 1979. v + 36pp. (0 11 340689 4).

50. *Crime and the community. John Croft. 1979. v + 16pp. (0 11 340690 8).

51. Life-sentence prisoners. David Smith (editor), Christopher Brown, Joan Worth, Roger Sapsford and Charlotte Banks (contributors). 1979. iv + 51pp. (0 11 340691 6).

52. *Hostels for offenders. Jane E. Andrews, with an appendix by Bill Sheppard. 1979. v + 30pp. (0 11 340692 4).

53. *Previous convictions, sentence and reconviction: a statistical study of a sample of 5,000 offenders convicted in January 1971. G. J. O. Phillpotts and L. B. Lancucki. 1979. v + 55pp.

54. *Sexual offences, consent and sentencing. Roy Walmsley and Karen White. 1979. vi + 77pp. (0 11 340694 0).

55. Crime prevention and the police. John Burrows, Paul Ekblom and Kevin Heal. 1979. v + 37pp. (0 11 340695 9).

56. *Sentencing practice in magistrates' courts. Roger Tarling, with the assistance of Mollie Weatheritt. 1979. vii + 54pp. (0 11 340696 7).

57. *Crime and comparative research. John Croft. 1979. iv + 16pp. (0 11 340697 5).

58. *Race, crime and arrests. Philip Stevens and Carole F. Willis. 1979. v + 69pp. (0 11 340698 3).

59. *Research and criminal policy. John Croft. 1980. iv + 14pp. (0 11 340699 1).

60. *Junior attendance centres. Anne B. Dunlop. 1980. v + 47pp. (0 11 340700 9).

61. *Police interrogation: an observational study in four police stations. Paul Softley, with the assistance of David Brown, Bob Forde, George Mair and David Moxon. 1980. vii + 67pp. (0 11 340701 7).

62. *Co-ordinating crime prevention efforts. F. J. Gladstone. 1980. v + 74pp. (0 11 340702 5).

63. *Crime prevention publicity: an assessment. D. Riley and P. Mayhew. 1980. v + 47pp. (0 11 340703 3).

64. *Taking offenders out of circulation. Stephen Brody and Roger Tarling. 1980. v + 46pp. (0 11 340704 1).

65. *Alcoholism and social policy: are we on the right lines? Mary Tuck. 1980. v + 30pp. (0 11 340705 X).

66. *Persistent petty offenders. Suzan Fairhead. 1981. vi + 78pp. (0 11 340706 8).

67. *Crime control and the police. Pauline Morris and Kevin Heal. 1981. v + 71pp. (0 11 340707 6).

68. *Ethnic minorities in Britain: a study of trends in their position since 1961. Simon Field, George Mair, Tom Rees and Philip Stevens. 1981. v + 48pp. (0 11 340708 4).

69. *Managing criminological research. John Croft. 1981. iv + 17pp. (0 11 340709 2).

70. *Ethnic minorities, crime and policing: a survey of the experiences of West Indians and whites. Mary Tuck and Peter Southgate. 1981. iv + 54pp. (0 11 340765 3).

71. *Contested trials in magistrates' courts. Julie Vennard. 1982. v + 32pp. (0 11 340766 1).

72. *Public disorder: a review of research and a study in one inner city area. Simon Field and Peter Southgate. 1982. v + 77pp. (0 11 340767 X).

73. *Clearing up crime. John Burrows and Roger Tarling. 1982. vii + 31pp. (0 11 340768 8).

74. *Residential burglary: the limits of prevention. Stuart Winchester and Hilary Jackson. 1982. v + 47pp. (0 11 340769 6).

75. *Concerning crime. John Croft. 1982. iv + 16pp. (0 11 340770 X).

76. *The British Crime Survey: first report. Mike Hough and Pat Mayhew. 1983. v + 62pp. (0 11 340786 6).

77. *Contacts between police and public: findings from the British Crime Survey. Peter Southgate and Paul Ekblom. 1984. v + 42pp. (0 11 340771 8).

78. *Fear of crime in England and Wales. Michael Maxfield. 1984. v + 57pp. (0 11 340772 6).

79. *Crime and police effectiveness. Ronald V. Clarke and Mike Hough 1984. iv + 33pp. (0 11 340773 3).

80. The attitudes of ethnic minorities. Simon Field. 1984. v + 49pp. (0 11 340774 2).

81. Victims of crime: the dimensions of risk. Michael Gottfredson. 1984. v + 54pp. (0 11 340775 0).

82. The tape recording of police interviews with suspects: an interim report. Carole Willis. 1984. v + 45pp. (0 11 340776 9).

83. Parental supervision and juvenile delinquency. David Riley and Margaret Shaw. 1985. v + 90pp. (0 11 340799 8).

84. Adult prisons and prisoners in England and Wales 1970–1982: a review of the findings of social research. Joy Mott. 1985. vi + 73pp. (0 11 340801 3).

85. Taking account of crime: key findings from the 1984 British Crime Survey. Mike Hough and Pat Mayhew. 1985. vi + 115pp. (0 11 341810 2).

86. Implementing crime prevention measures. Tim Hope. 1985. vi + 82pp. (0 11 340812 9).

87. Resettling refugees: the lessons of research. Simon Field. 1985. vi + 66pp. (0 11 340815 3).

88. Investigating burglary: the measurement of police performance. John Burrows. 1986. vi + 36pp. (0 11 340824 2).

89. Personal violence. Roy Walmsley. 1986. vi + 87pp. (0 11 340827 7).

90. Police-public encounters. Peter Southgate. 1986. vi + 150pp. (0 11 340834 X).

91. Grievance procedures in prisons. John Ditchfield and Claire Austin. 1986. vi + 87pp. (0 11 340839 0).

92. The effectiveness of the Forensic Science Service. Malcolm Ramsay. 1987. v + 100pp. (0 11 340842 0).

93. The police complaints procedure: a survey of complainant's views. David Brown. 1987. v + 98pp. (0 11 340853 6).

94. The validity of the reconviction prediction score. Denis Ward. 1987. vi + 46. (0 11 340882 X).

95. Economic aspects of the illicit drug market enforcement policies in the United Kingdom. Adam Wagstaff and Alan Maynard. 1988. vii + 156pp. (0 11 340883 8).

96. Schools, disruptive behaviour and deliquency: a review of literature. John Graham. 1988. v + 70pp. (0 11 340887 0).

97. The tape recording of police interviews with suspects: a second interim report. Carole Willis, John Macleod and Peter Naish. 1988. vii + 97pp. (o 11 340890 0).

98. Triable-either-way cases: Crown Court or magistrate's court. David Riley and Julie Vennard. 1988. v + 52pp. (0 11 340891 9).

99. Directing patrol work: a study of uniformed policing. John Burrows and Helen Lewis. 1988 v + 66pp. (0 11 340891 9).

100. Probation day centres. George Mair. 1988. v + 44pp. (0 11 340894 3).

101. Amusement machines: dependency and delinquency. John Graham. 1988. v + 48pp. (0 11 340895 1).

102. The use and enforcement of compensation orders in magistrates' courts. Tim Newburn. 1988. v + 49pp. (0 11 340 896 X).

103. Sentencing practice in the Crown Court, David Moxon. 1988. v + 90pp. (0 11 340902 8).

104. Detention at the police station under the police and Criminal Evidence Act 1984. David Brown. 1988. v + 88pp. (0 11 340908 7).

105. Changes in rape offences and sentencing. Charles Lloyd and Roy Walmsley. 1989. vi + 53pp. (0 11 340910 9).

106. Concerns about rape. Lorna Smith. 1989. v + 48pp. (0 11 340911 7).

107. Domestic violence. Lorna Smith. 1989. v + 132pp. (0 11 340925 7).

108. Drinking and disorder: a study of non-metropolitan violence. Mary Tuck. 1989. v + 111pp. (0 11 340926 5).

109. Special security units. Roy Walmsley. 1989. v + 114pp. (0 11 340961 3).

110. Pre-trial delay: the implications of time limits. Patricia Morgan and Julie Vennard. 1989. v + 66pp. (0 11 340964 8).

111. The 1988 British Crime Survey. Pat Mayhew, David Elliott and Lizanne Dowds. 1989. v + 133pp. (0 11 340965 6).

112. The settlement of claims at the Criminal Injuries Compensation Board. Tim Newburn. 1989. v + 40pp. (0 11 340967 2).

113. Race, community groups and service delivery. Hilary Jackson and Simon Field. 1989. v + 62pp. (0 11 340972 9).

114. Money payment supervision orders: probation policy and practice. George Mair and Charles Lloyd. 1989. v + 40pp. (0 11 340971 0).

115. Suicide and self-injury in prison: a literature review. Charles Lloyd. 1990. v + 69pp. (0 11 3409745 5).

116. Keeping in Touch: police-victim communication in two areas. Tim Newburn and Susan Merry. 1990. v + 52pp. (0 11 340974 5).

117. The police and public in England and Wales: a British Crime Survey report. Wesley G. Skogan. 1990. vi + 74pp. (0 11 340995 8).

118. Control in prisons: a review of the literature. John Ditchfield. 1990. (0 11 340996 6).

119. Trends in crime and their interpretation: a study of recorded crime in post-war England and Wales. Simon Field. 1990. (0 11 340994 X).

120. Electronic monitoring: the trials and their results. George Mair and Claire Nee. 1990. v + 79pp. (0 11 340998 2).

121. Drink driving: the effects of enforcement. David Riley. 1991. viii + 78pp. (0 11 340999 0).

122. Managing difficult prisoners: the Parkhurst Special Unit. Roy Walmsley (Ed.) 1991. x + 139pp. (0 11 341008 5).

123. Investigating burglary: the effects of PACE. David Brown. 1991. xii + 106pp. (0 11 34011 5).

124. Traffic policing in changing times. Peter Southgate and Catriona Mirlees-Black. 1991. viii + 139pp. (0 11 341019 0).

125. Magistrates' court or Crown Court? mode of trial decisions and sentencing. Carol Hedderman and David Moxon. 1992. vii + 53pp. (0 11 341036 0).

126. Developments in the use of compensation orders in magistrates' courts since October 1988. David Moxon, John Martin Corkery and Carol Hedderman. 1992. x + 48pp. (0 11 341042 5).

ALSO

Designing out crime. R. V. G. Clarke and P. Mayhew (editors). 1980. viii + 186pp. (0 11 340732 7).
(This book collects, with an introduction, studies taht were originally published in HORS 34, 47, 49, 55, 62 and 63 and which are illustrative of the 'situational' approach to crime prevention.)

Policing today. Kevin Heal, Roger Tarling and John Burrows (editors). v + 181pp. (0 11 340800 5).
(This book brings together twelve separate studies on police matters produced during the last few years by the Unit. The collection records some relatively little known contributions to the debate on policing.)

Managing Criminal Justice: a collection of papers. David Moxon (ed.). 1985. vi + 222pp. (0 11 340811 0).
(This book brings together a number of studies bearing on the management of the criminal justice system. It includes papers by social scientists and operational researchers working within the Research and Planning Unit, and academic researchers who have studied particular aspects of the criminal process.)

Situational Crime Prevention: from theory into practice. Kevin Heal and Gloria Laycock (editors). 1986. vii + 166pp. (0 11 340826 9).
(Following the publication of *Designing Out Crime*, further research has been completed on the theoretical background to crime prevention. In drawing this work together this book sets down some of the theoretical concerns and discusses the emerging practical issues. It includes contributions by Unit staff as well as academics from this country and abroad).

Communities and crime reduction. Tim Hope and Margaret Shaw (eds.). 1988. vii + 311pp. (11 340892 7).
(The central theme of this book is the possibility of preventing crime by building upon the resources of local communities and of active citizens. The specially commissioned chapters, by distinguished international authors, review contemporary research and policy on community crime prevention.)

New directions in police training. Peter Southgate (ed.). 1988. xi + 256pp. (11 340889 7).
(Training is central to the development of the police role, and particular thought and effort now go into making it more responsive current needs—in order to produce police officers who are both effective and sensitive in their dealing with the public. This book illustrates some of the thinking and research behind these developments.)

The above HMSO publications can be purchased from Government Bookshops or through booksellers.

The following Home Office research publications available on request form the Home Office Research and Planning Unit, 50 Queen Anne's Gate, London SW1H 9AT.

Research Unit Papers (RUP)

1. Uniformed police work and management technology. J. M. Hough. 1980.
2. Supplementary information on sexual offences and sentencing. Roy Walmsley and Karen White. 1980.
3. Board of visitor adjudications. David Smith, Claire Austin and John Ditchfield. 1981.
4. Day centres and probation. Suzan Fairhead, with the assistance of J. Wilkinson-Grey. 1981.

Research and Planning Unit Papers (RPUP)

5. Ethnic minorities and complaints against the police. Philip Stevens and Carole Willis. 1982.
6. *Crime and public housing. Mike Hough and Pat Mayhew (editors). 1982.
7. *Abstracts of race relations research. George Mair and Philip Stevens (editors). 1982.
8. Police probationer training in race relations. Peter Southgate. 1982.
9. *The police response to calls from the public. Paul Ekblom and Kevin Heal. 1982.
10. City centre crime: a situational approach to prevention. Malcolm Ramsay. 1982.
11. Burglary in schools: the prospects for prevention. Tim Hope. 1982.
12. *Fine enforcement. Paul Softley and David Moxon. 1982.
13. Vietnamese refugees. Peter Jones. 1982.
14. Community resources for victims of crime. Karen Williams. 1983.
15. The use, effectiveness and impact of police stop and search powers. Carole Willis. 1983.
16. Acquittal rates. Sid Butler. 1983.
17. Criminal justice comparisons: the case of Scotland and England and Wales. Lorna J. F. Smith. 1983.
18. Time taken to deal with juveniles under criminal proceedings. Catherine Frankenburg and Roger Tarling. 1983.
19. Civilian review of complaints against the police: a survey of the United States literature. David C. Brown. 1983.
20. Police action on motoring offences. David Riley. 1983.
21. *Diverting drunks from the criminal justice system. Sue Kingsley and George Mair. 1983.
22. The staff resource implications of an independent prosecution system. Peter R. Jones. 1983.
23. Reducing the prison population: an exploratory study in Hampshire. David Smith, Bill Sheppard, George Mair, Karen Williams. 1984.
24. Criminal justice system model: magistrates' courts sub-model. Susan Rice. 1984.
25. Measures of police effectiveness and efficiency. Ian Sinclair and Clive Miller. 1984.
26. Punishment practice by prison Boards of Visitors. Susan Iles, Adrienne Connors, Chris May, Joy Mott. 1984.
27. *Reparation, conciliation and mediation: current projects and plans in England and Wales. Tony Marshall. 1984.
28. Magistrates' domestic courts: new perspectives. Tony Marshall (editor). 1984.
29. Racism awareness training for the police. Peter Southgate. 1984.
30. Community constables: a study of a policing initiative. David Brown and Susan Iles. 1985.
31. Recruiting volunteers. Hilary Jackson. 1985.
32. Juvenile sentencing: is there a tariff? David Moxon, Peter Jones, Roger Tarling. 1985.
33. Bringing people together: mediation and reparation projects in Great Britain. Tony Marshall and Martin Walpole. 1985.
34. Remands in the absence of the accused. Chris May. 1985.
35. Modelling the criminal justice system. Patricia M. Morgan. 1985.
36. The criminal justice system model: the flow model. Hugh Pullinger 1986.
37. Burglary: police actions and victim views. John Burrows. 1986.

38. Unlocking community resources: four experimental government small grants schemes. Hilary Jackson. 1986.

39. The cost of discriminating: a review of the literature. Shirley Dex. 1986.

40. Waiting for Crown Court trial: the remand population. Rachel Pearce. 1987.

41. Children's evidence the need for corroboration. Carol Hedderman. 1987.

42. A preliminary study of victim offender mediation and reparation schemes in England & Wales. Gwynn Davis, Jacky Boucherat, David Watson, Adrian Thatcher (Consultant). 1987.

43. Explaining fear of crime: evidence from the 1984 British Crime Survey. Michael Maxfield. 1987.

44. Judgements of crime seriousness: evidence from the 1984 British Crime Survey. Ken Pease. 1988.

45. Waiting time on the day in magistrates' courts: a review of case listings practises. David Moxon and Roger Tarling (editors). 1988.

46. Bail and probation work: the ILPS temporary bail action project. George Mair. 1988.

47. Police work and manpower allocation. Roger Tarling. 1988.

48. Computers in the courtroom. Carol Hedderman. 1988.

49. Data interchange between magistrates' courts and other agencies. Carol Hedderman. 1988.

50. Bail and probation work II: the use of London probation/bail hostels for bailees. Helen Lewis and George Mair. 1989.

51. The role and function of police community liaison officers. Susan V. Phillips and Raymond Cochrane. 1989.

52. Insuring against burglary losses. Helen Lewis. 1989.

53. Remand decisions in Brighton and Bournemouth. Patricia Morgan and Rachel Pearce. 1989.

54. Racially motivated incidents reported to the police. Jayne Seagrave. 1989.

55. Review of research on re-offending of mentally disordered offenders. David J. Murray. 1990.

56. Risk prediction and probation: papers from a Research and Planning Unit workshop. George Mair (editor). 1990.

57. Household fires: findings from the British Crime Survey 1988. Chris May. 1990.

58. Home Office funding of victim support schemes—money well spent?. Justin Russell. 1990.

59. Unit fines: experiments in four courts. David Moxon, Mike Sutton and Carol Hedderman. 1990.

60. Deductions from benefit for fine default. David Moxon, Carol Hedderman and Mike Sutton. 1990.

61. Monitoring time limits on custodial remands. Paul F. Henderson. 1991.

62. Remands in custody for up to 28 days: the experiments. Paul F. Henderson and Patricia Morgan. 1991.

63. Parenthood training for young offenders: an evaluation of courses in Young Offender Institutions. Diane Caddle. 1991.

64. The multi-agency approach in practice: the North Plaistow racial harassment project. Wiliam Saulsbury and Benjamin Bowling. 1991.

65. Offending while on bail: a survey of recent studies. Patricia M. Morgan. 1992.

66. Juveniles sentenced for serious offences: a comparison of regimes in Young Offender Institutions and Local Authority Community Homes. John Ditchfield and Liza Catan. 1992.

67. The management and deployment of police armed response vehicles. Peter Southgate. 1992.

68. Using psychometric personality tests in the selection of firearms officers. Catriona Mirrlees-Black. 1992.

69. Bail information schemes: practice and effect. Charles Lloyd. 1992.

70. Crack and cocaine in England and Wales. Joy Mott (editor). 1992.

Research Bulletin

The Research Bulletin is published twice a year and consists mainly of short articles relating to projects which are part of the Home Office Research and Planning Unit's research programme.

Printed in the United Kingdom for HMSO
Dd297219 2/93 C15 G531 10170